Flowers in the Wild Journal

DORIS LANCE

ISBN: 978-1-63950-051-2 (sc)
ISBN: 978-1-63950-052-9 (e)

Gateway Towards Success

8063 MADISON AVE #1252
Indianapolis, IN 46227
+13176596889
www.writersapex.com

Flowers in the Wild

CAPTURE YOUR DAYS IN WORDS AND PICTURES

Question #1: What do you wish you had more time to do?

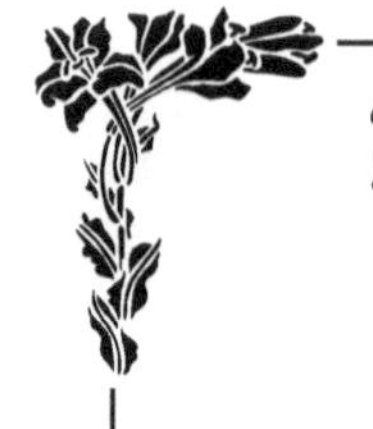

"As water reflects the face, so
one's life reflects the heart."

Proverbs 27:19 NIV

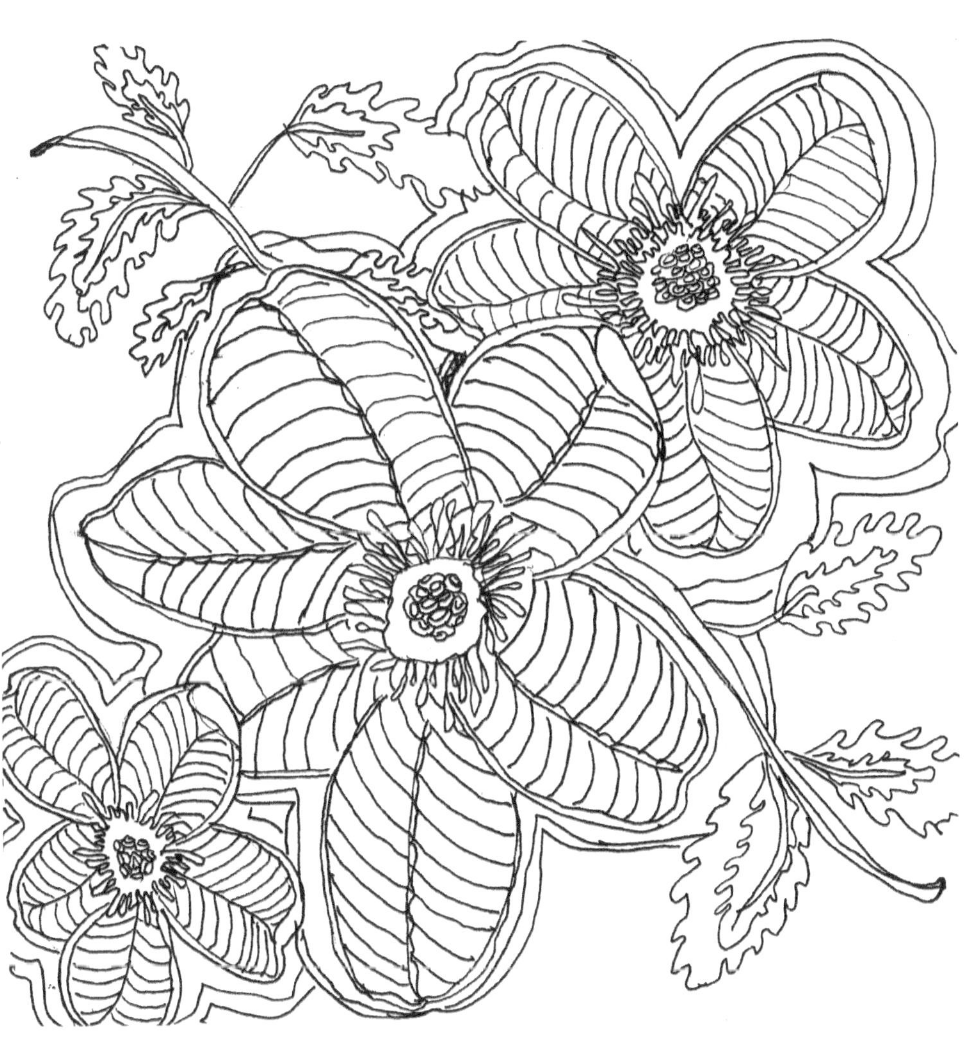

Question #2: What has been one of your proudest moments?

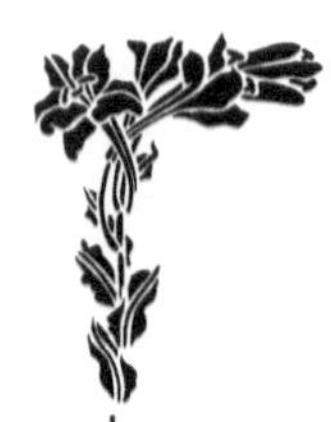

Gautama Buddha

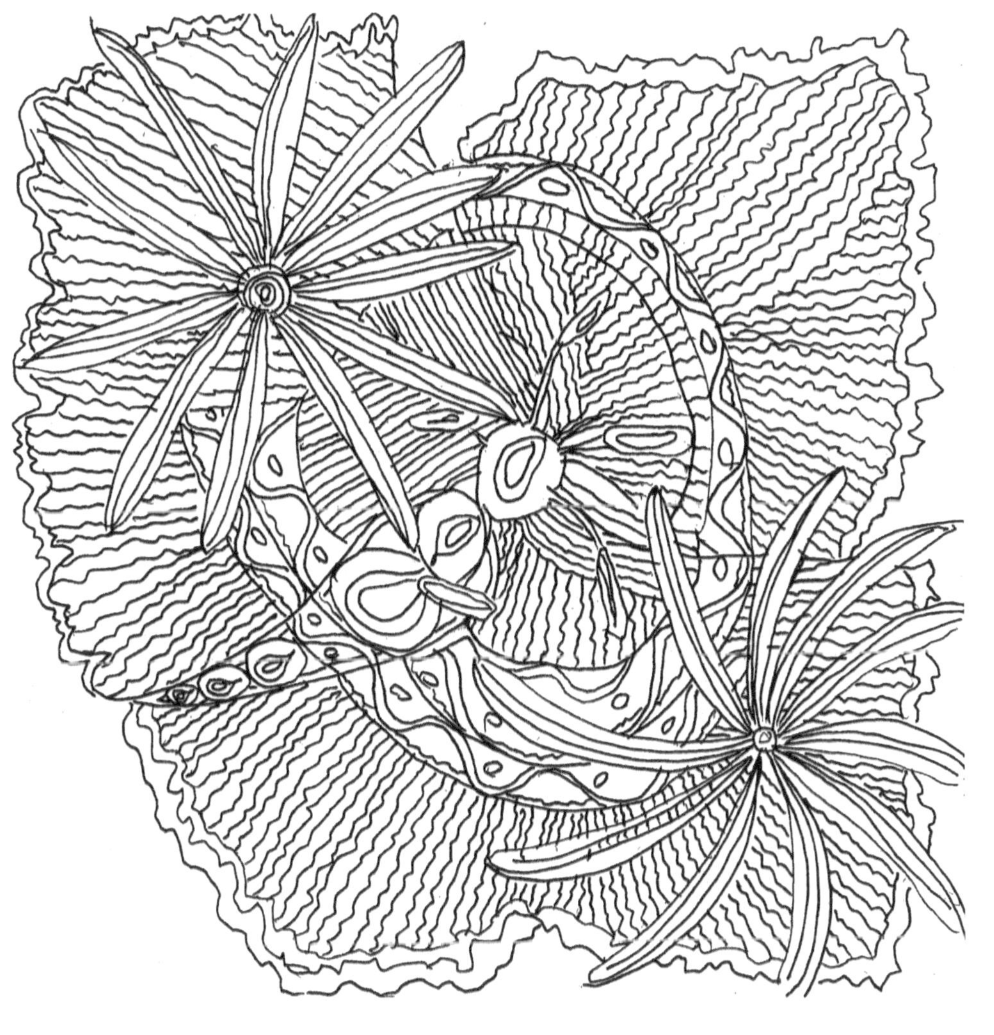

Question #3: How and when was the last time you pushed the boundaries of your comfort zone?

____

____

____

____

____

____

____

____

____

____

____

____

____

____

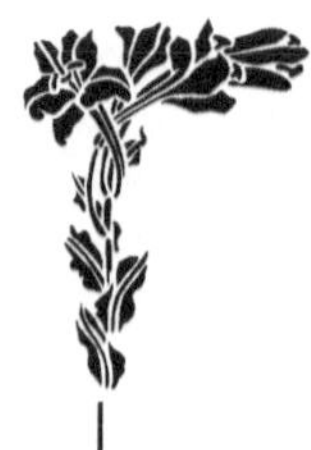

"We can never obtain peace in the outer world until we make peace with ourselves."

14th Dalai Lama

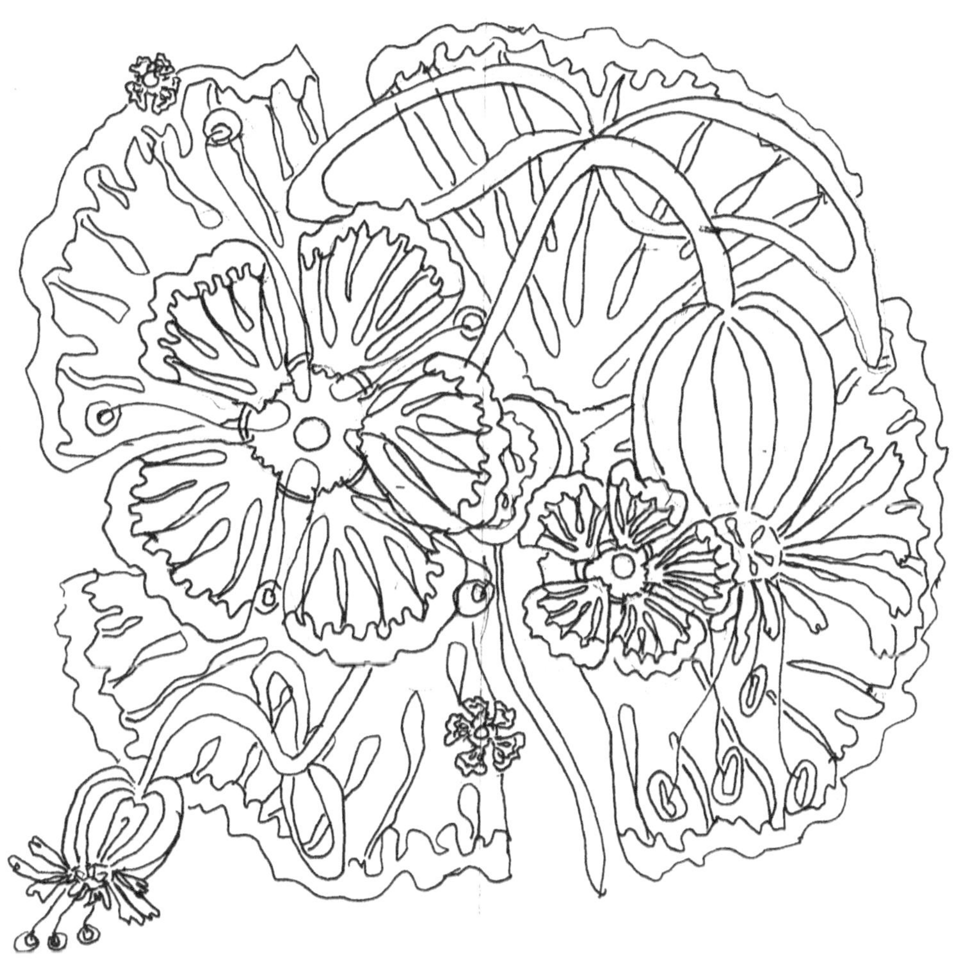

Question #4: What book has left a lasting impression on you?

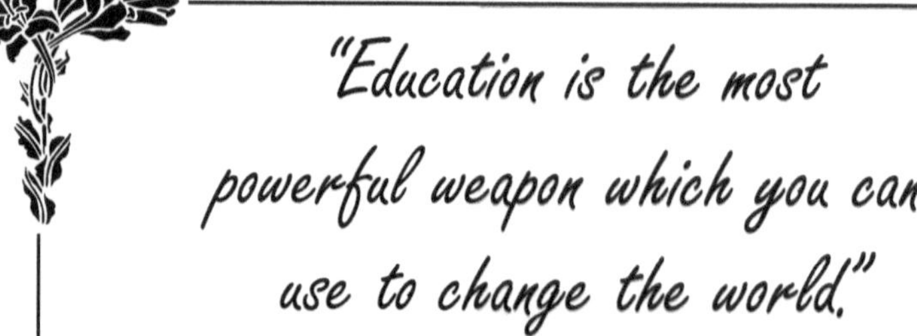

Nelson Mandela

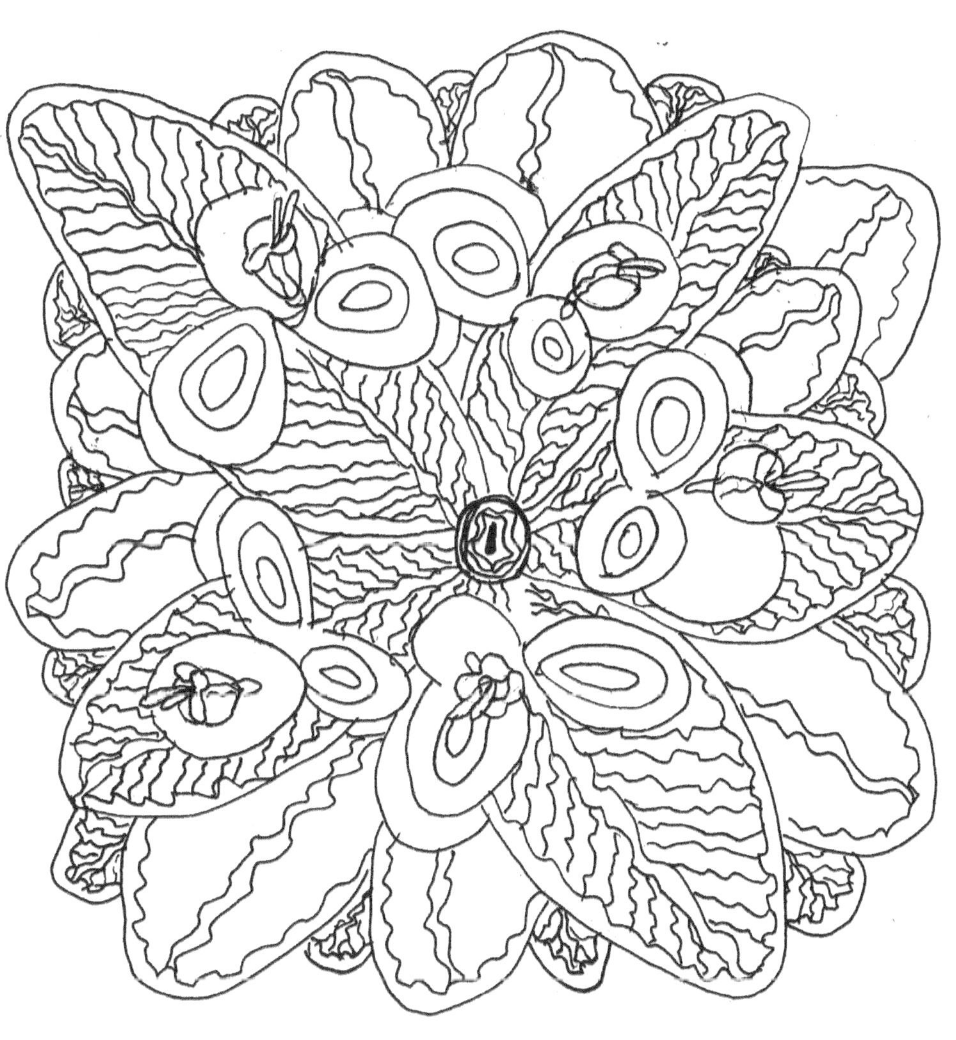

Question #5: What happened today that brought a smile on your face?

____

____

____

____

____

____

____

____

____

____

____

____

____

____

____

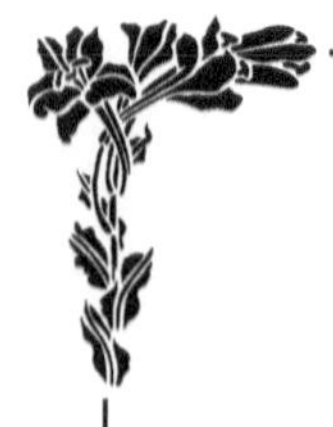

"Happiness is not something ready-made. It comes from your own actions."

14th Dalai Lama

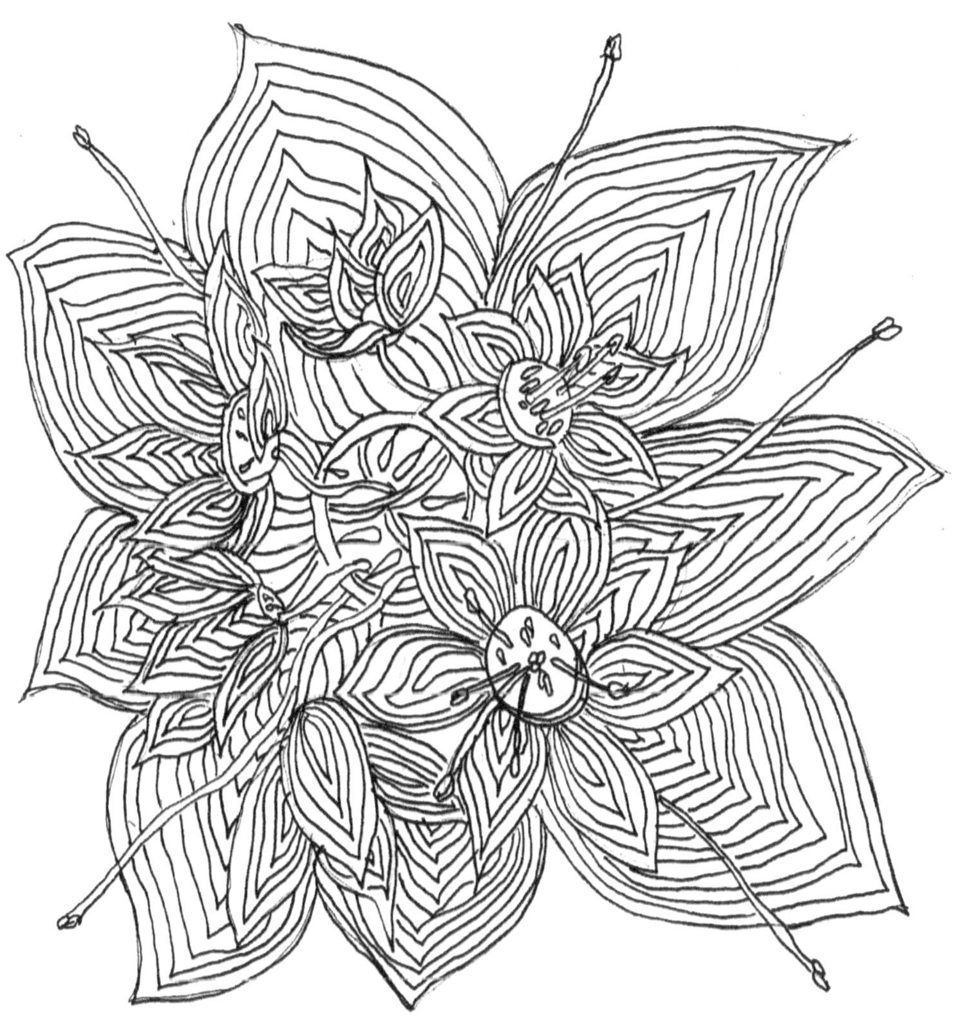

Question #6: How can you help others in your family, community, or at work?

____

____

____

____

____

____

____

____

____

____

____

____

____

____

____

> *"Being deeply loved by someone gives you strength, while loving someone deeply gives you courage."*
>
> Lao Tzu

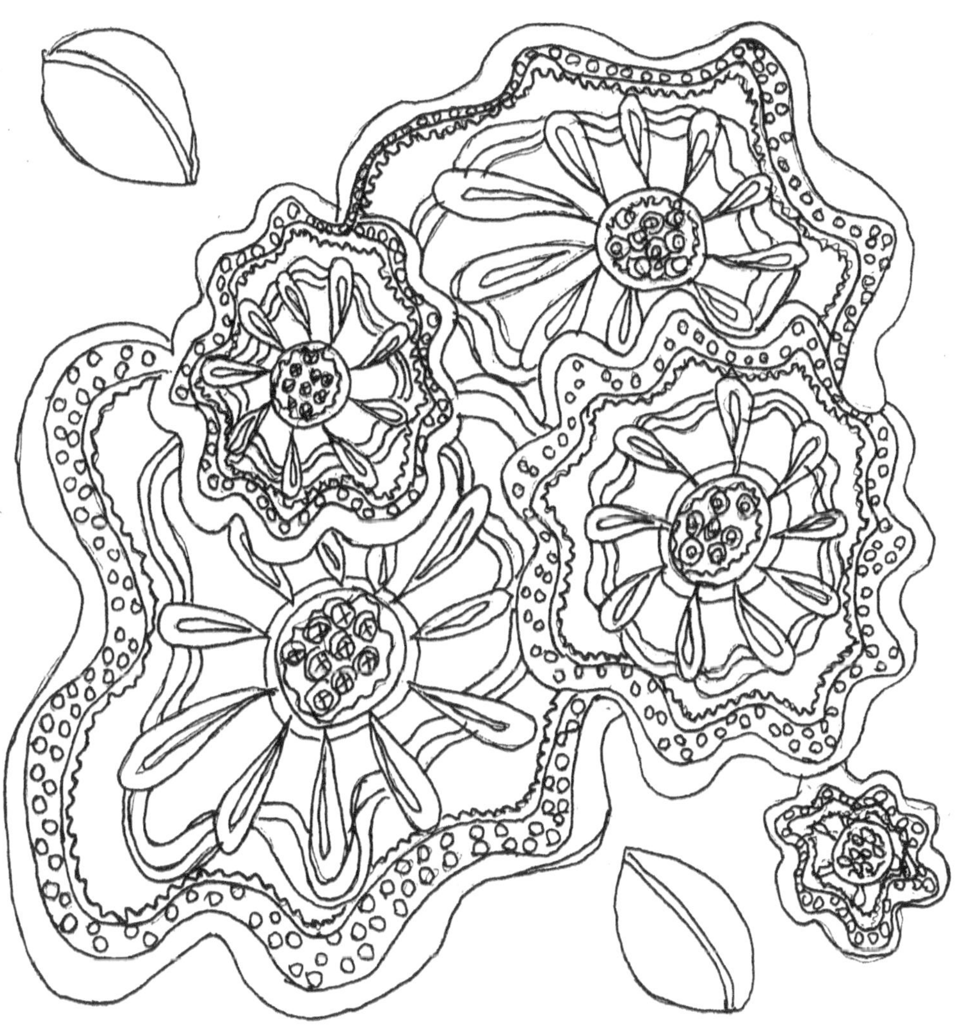

Question #7: What are your first thoughts when you wake up in the morning?

____

____

____

____

____

____

____

____

____

____

____

____

____

____

____

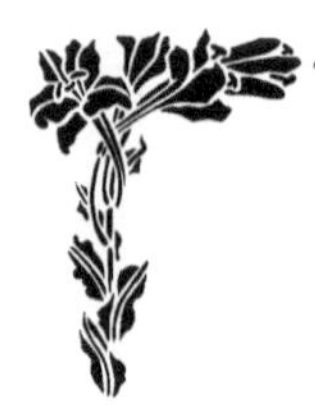

"Prayer is the key of the morning and the bolt of the evening."

Mahatma Gandhi

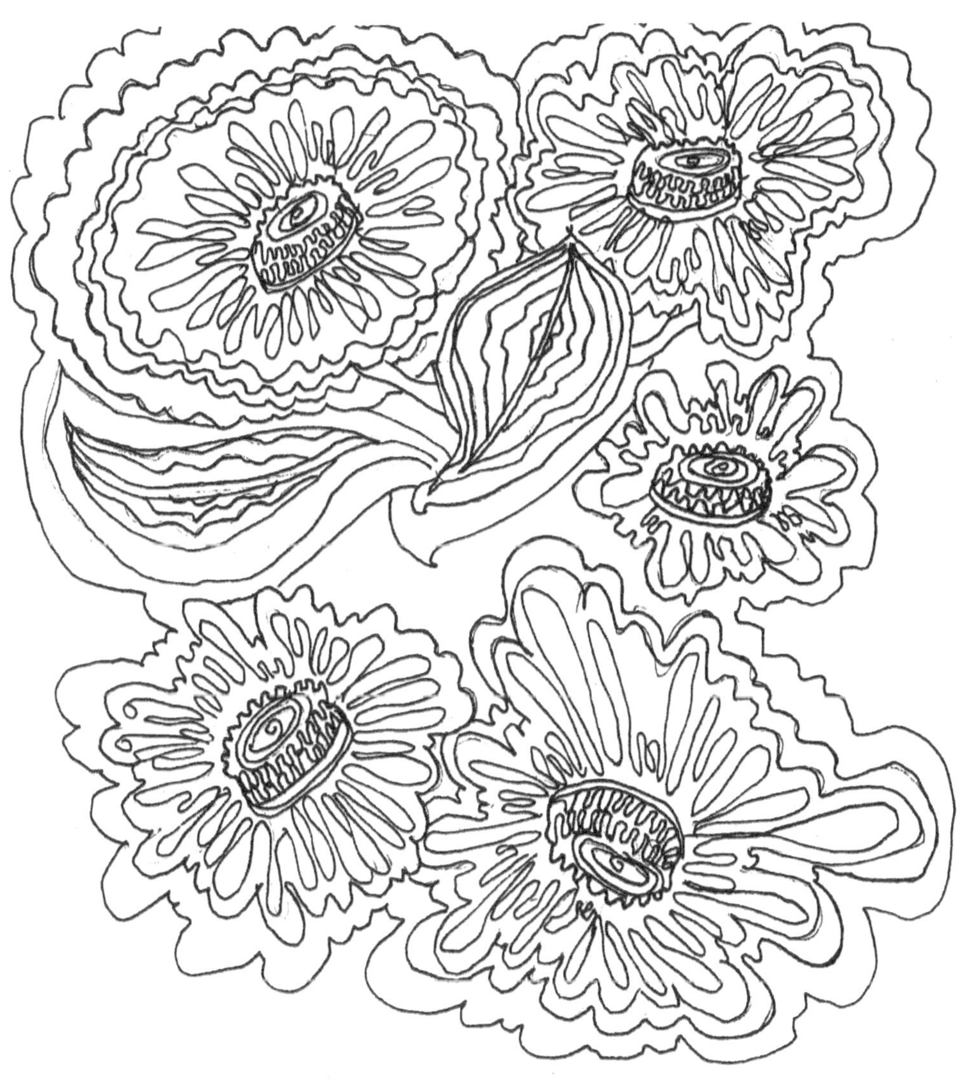

Question #8: How did you overcome one of the biggest challenges you have faced so far?

____

____

____

____

____

____

____

____

____

____

____

____

____

____

____

"Whoever walks in integrity walks secure, but whoever takes crooked paths will be found out."

Proverbs 10:9 NIV

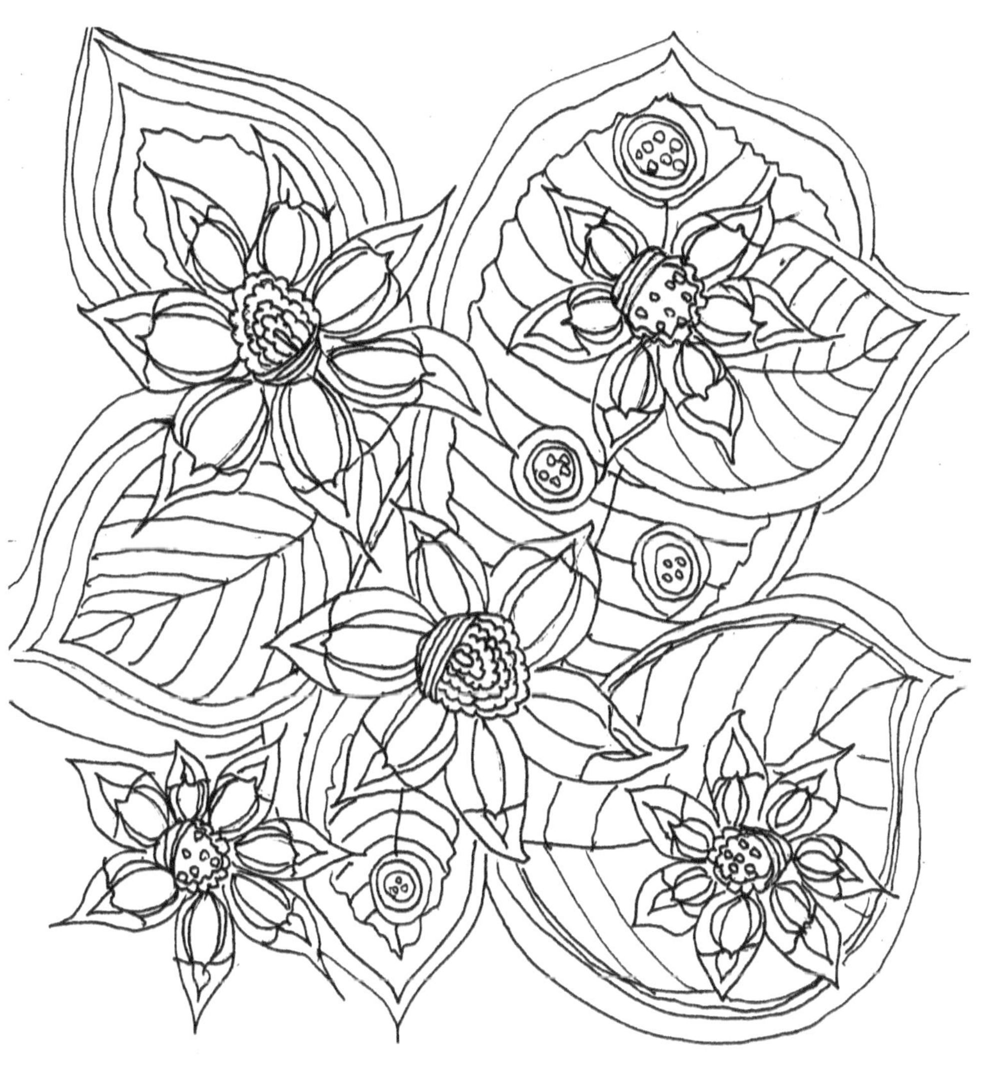

Question #9: If you could meet one person from history, who would it be? Why?

____

____

____

____

____

____

____

____

____

____

____

____

____

____

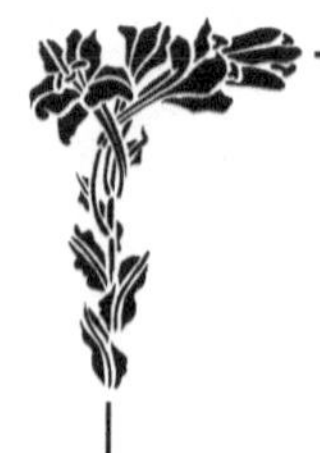

"Not all of us can do great things. But we can do small things with great love."

Mother Teresa

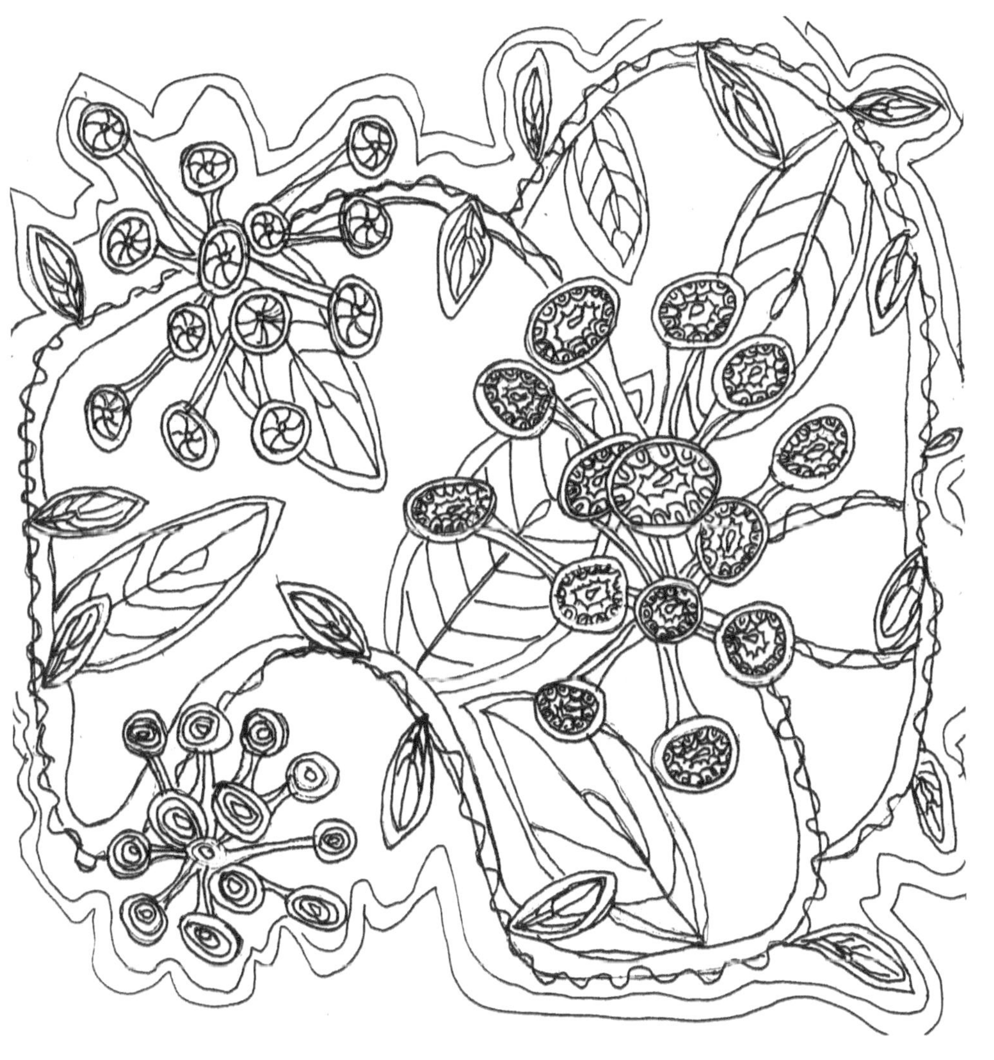

Question #10: What could you donate (time, money, talent, clothing) to help the less fortunate?

____

____

____

____

____

____

____

____

____

____

____

____

____

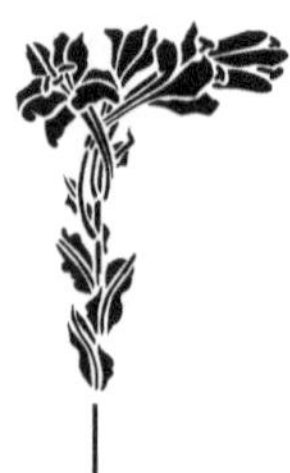

"For to be free is not merely to cast off one's chains, but to live in a way that respects and enhances the freedom of others."

Nelson Mandela

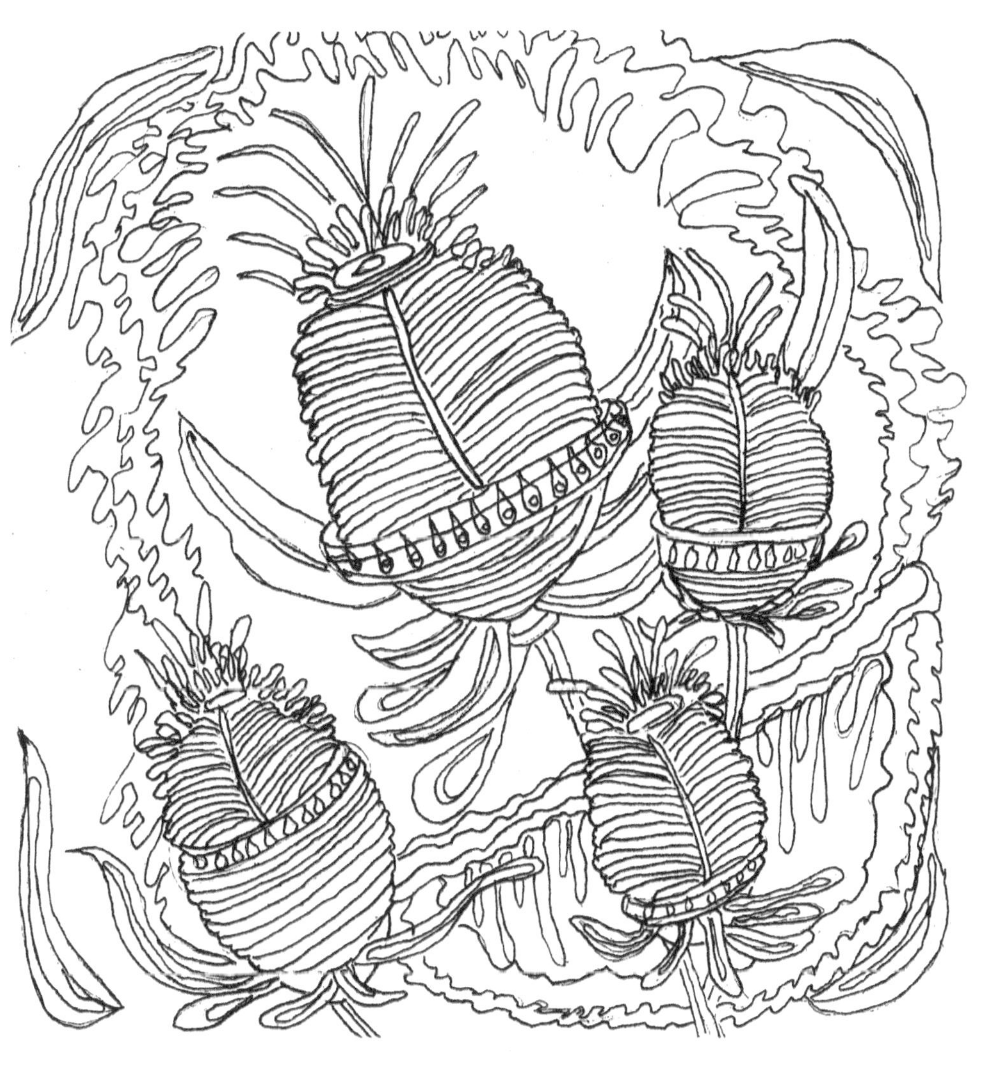

Question #11: Record a holiday memory that brings you joy and happiness?

____

____

____

____

____

____

____

____

____

____

____

____

____

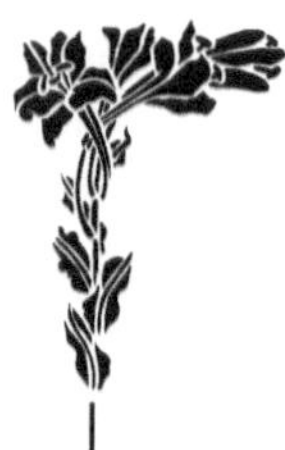

"Friends are companions on a journey, who ought to aid each other to preserver in a road to a happier life."

Pythagoras

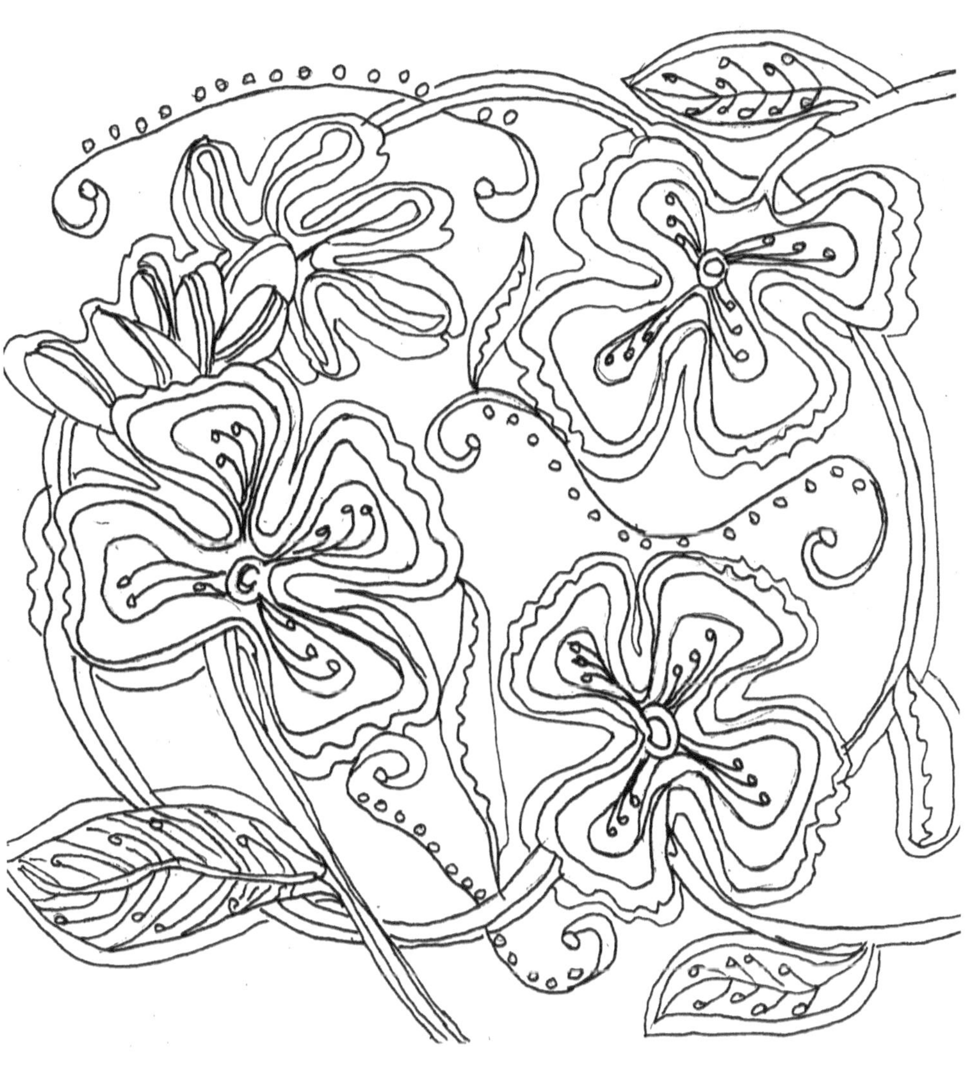

Question #12: What desires keep tugging at your heart?

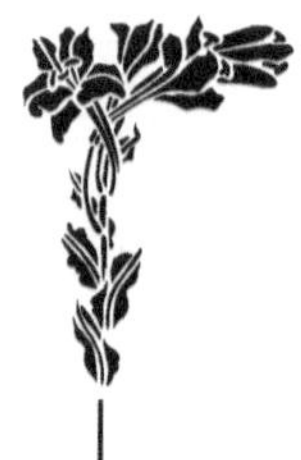

"Thoughts disentangle themselves when they pass through the lips and fingertips."

Dawson Trotman

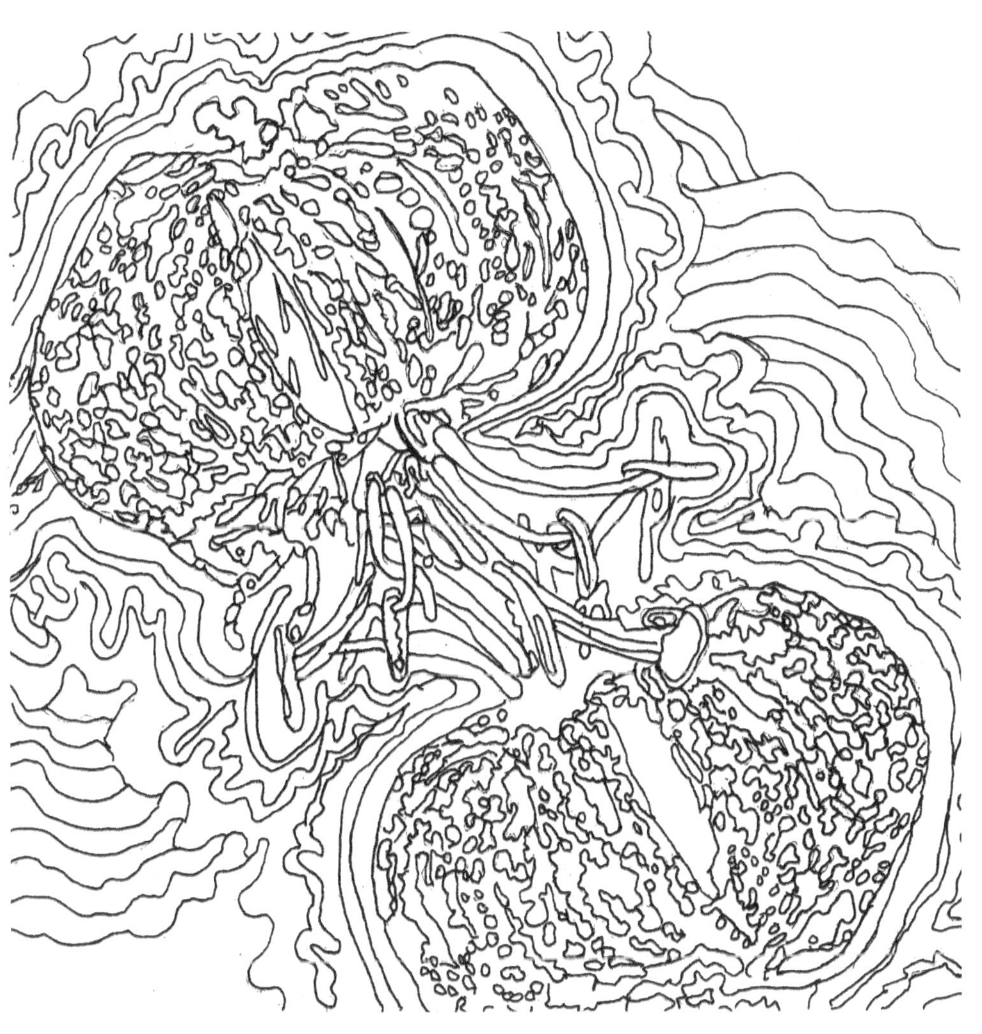

Question #13: What problem do you want/need to solve in the next six months?

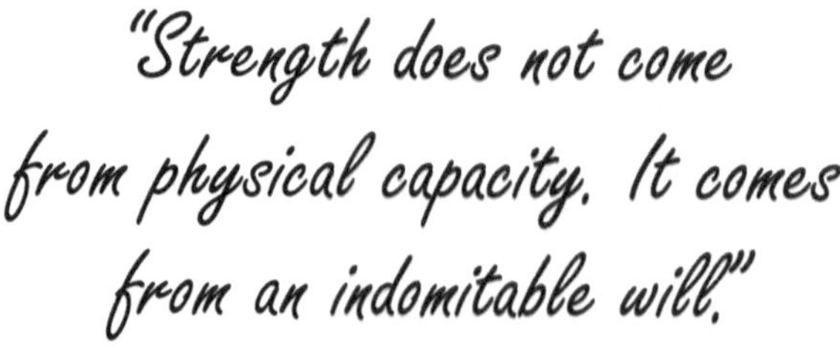

Mahatama Gandhi

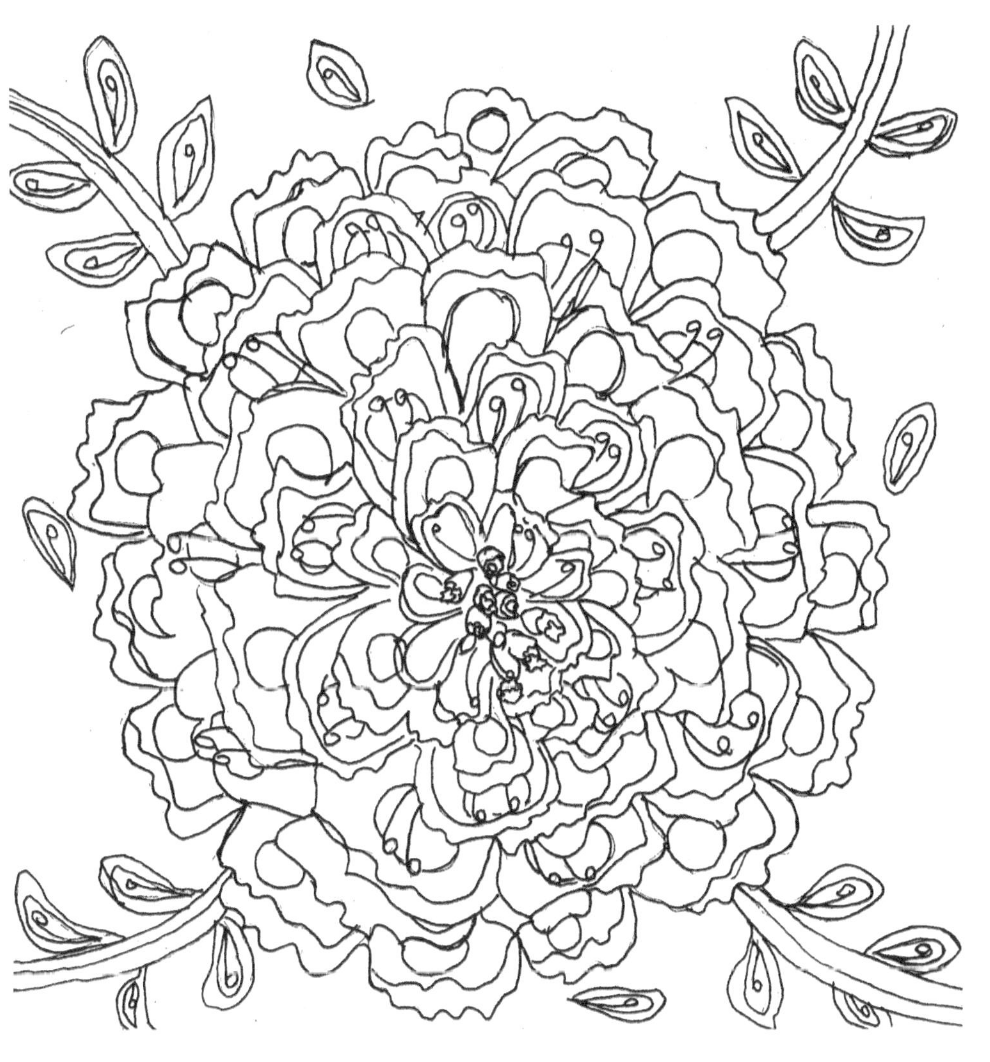

Question #14: What would you want others to know about you?

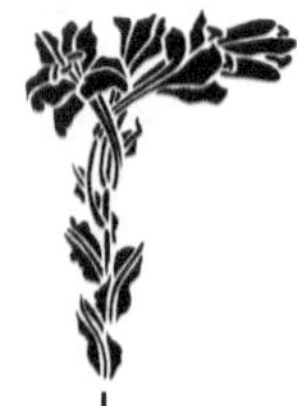

"*Anxiety weighs down the heart but a kind word cheers it up.*"

Proverbs 12:20 NIV

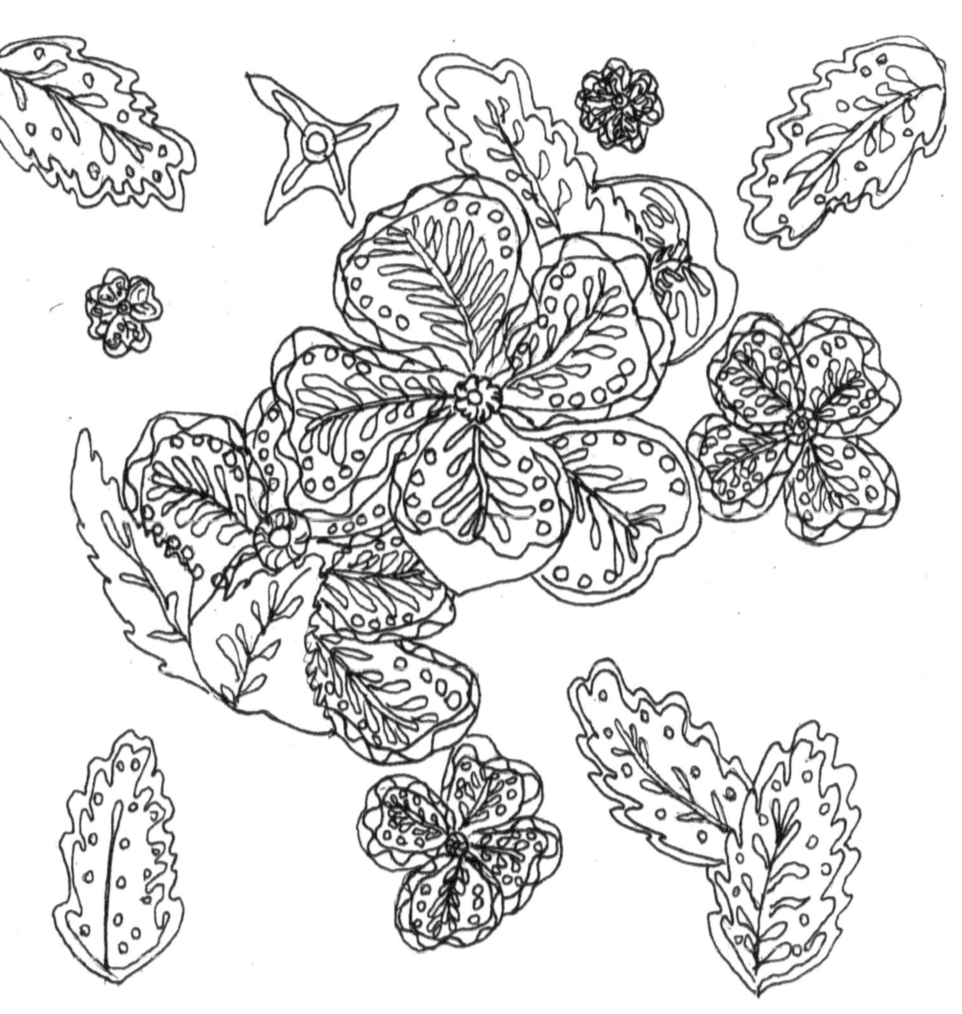

Question #15: When you get upset, what are the ways you deal with it?

____

____

____

____

____

____

____

____

____

____

____

____

____

____

____

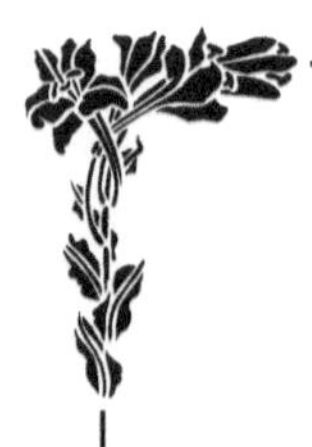

"Over every mountain there is a path although it may not be seen from the valley."

Theodore Roethke

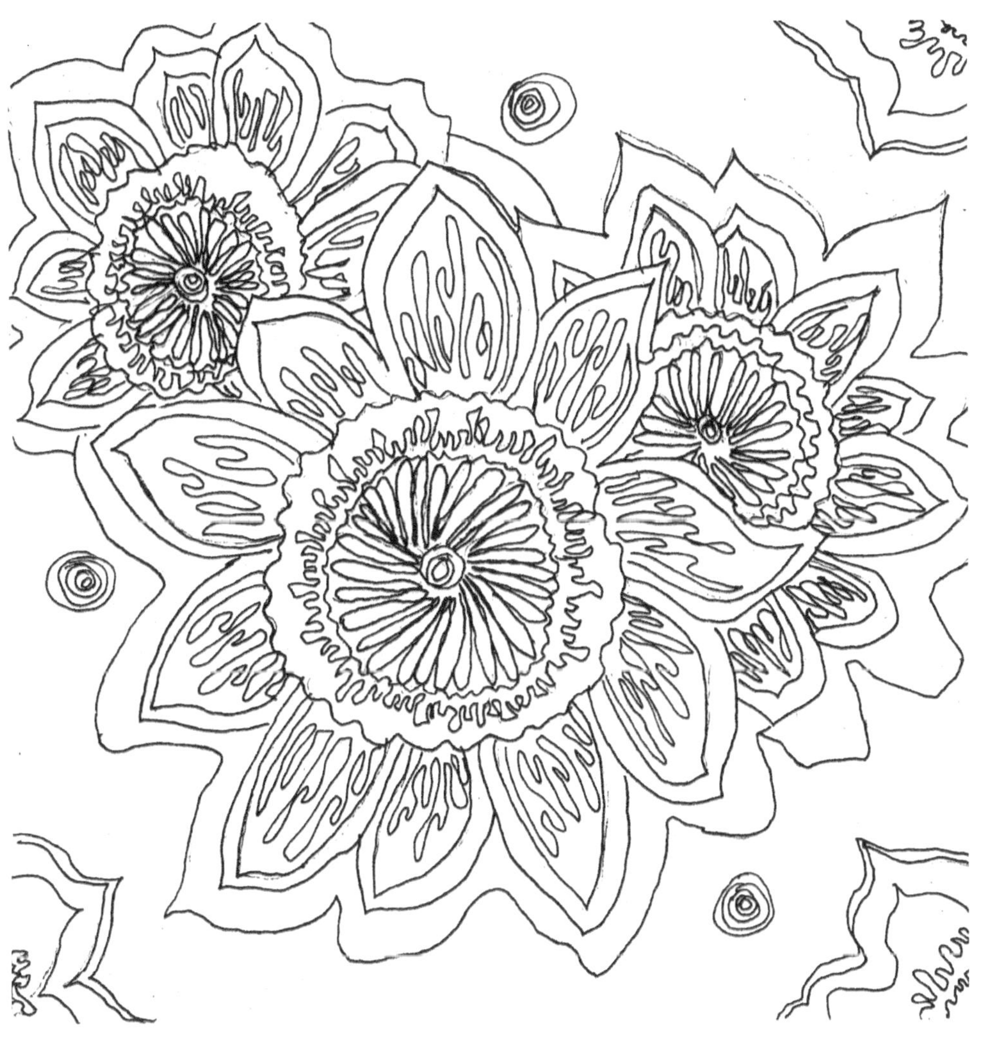

Question #16: What is missing in your life?

____

____

____

____

____

____

____

____

____

____

____

____

____

____

____

> *"Health is the greatest gift, contentment the greatest wealth, faithfulness the best relationship."*
>
> Gautama Buddha

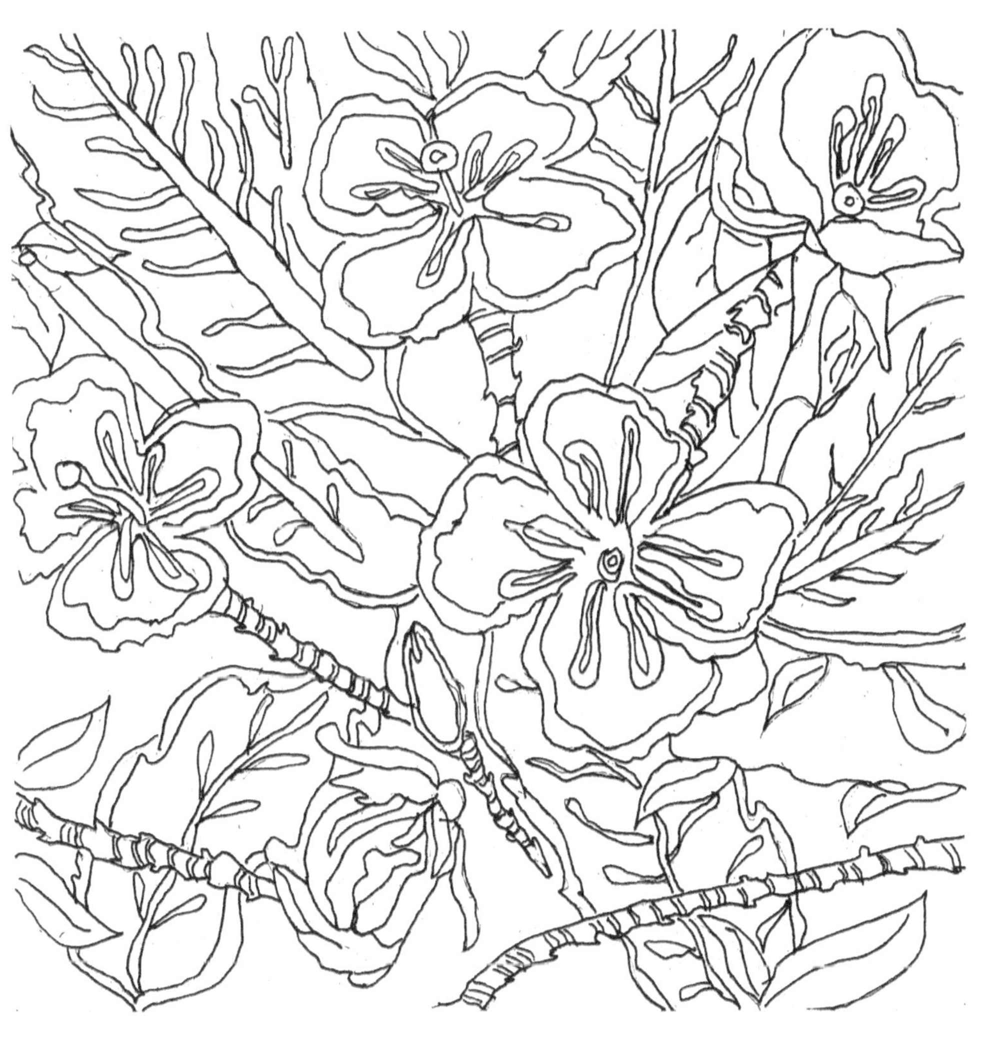

Question #17: How would you describe yourself?

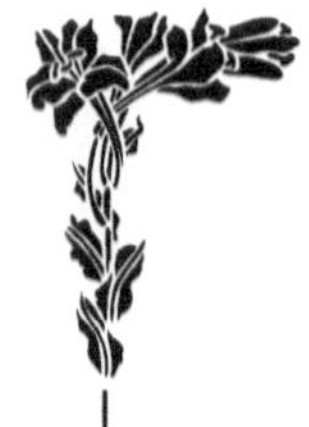

"A good head and a good heart are always a formidable combination."

Nelson Mandela

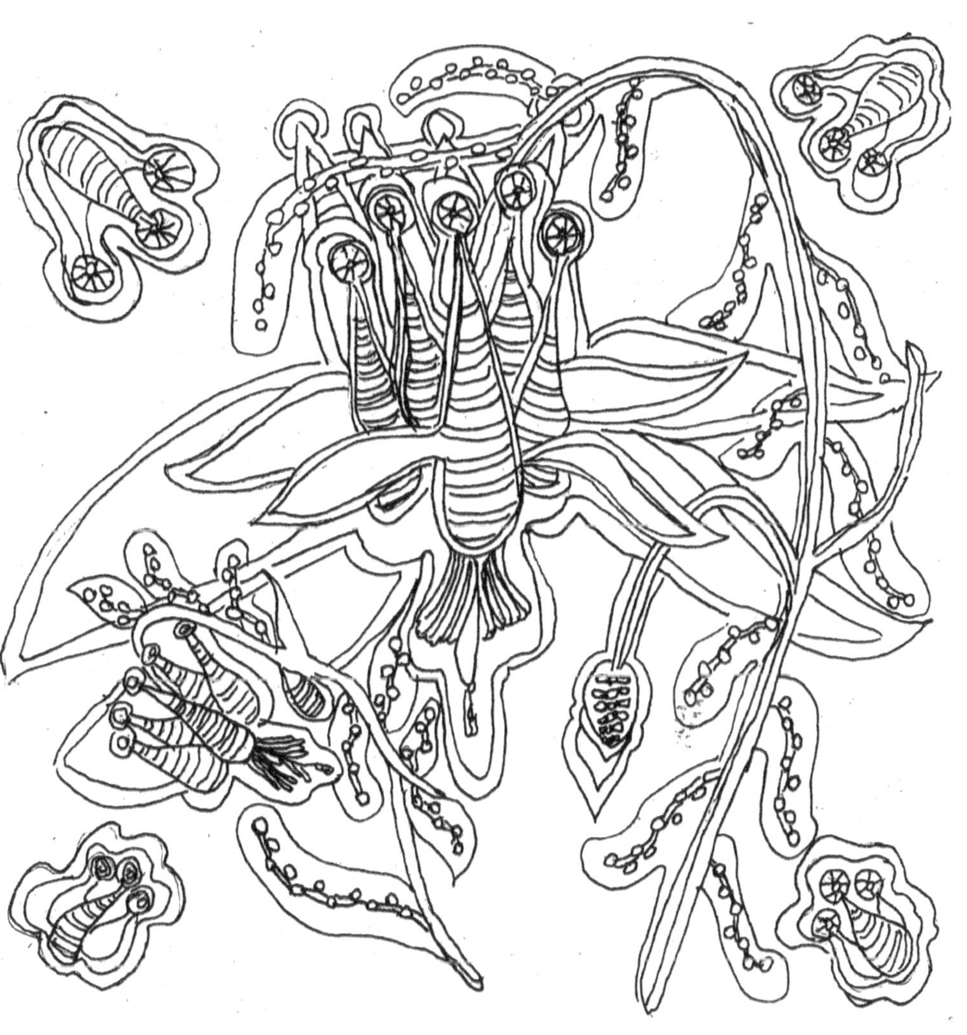

Question #18: Who are your heroes and why?

____

____

____

____

____

____

____

____

____

____

____

____

____

____

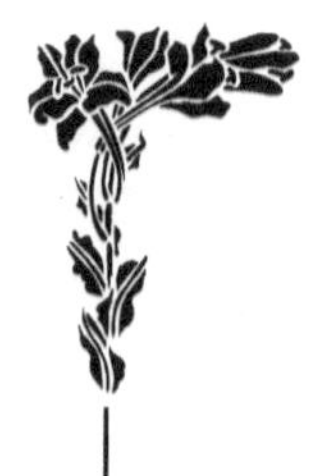

"If it is possible, as far as it depends on you, live at peace with everyone."

Romans 12:18 NIV

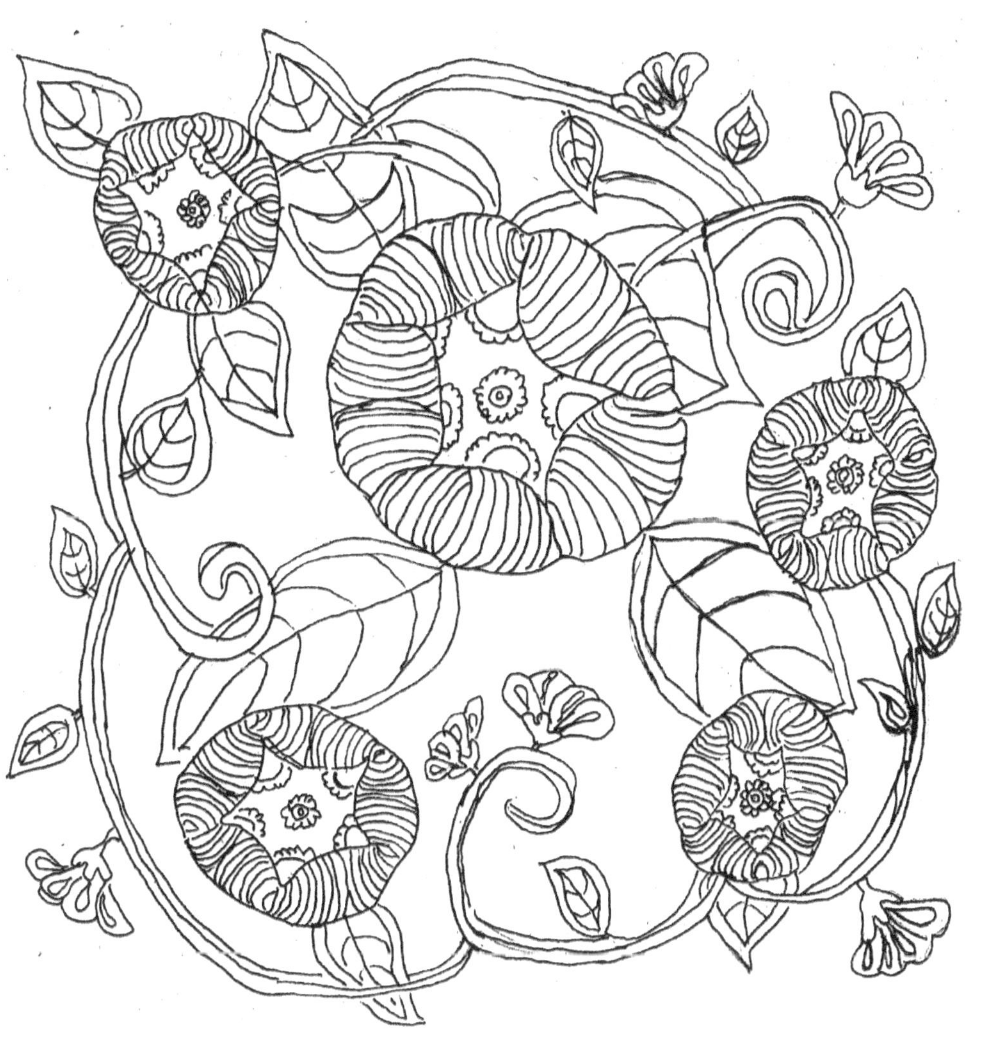

Question #19: What does unconditional love look like to you?

____

____

____

____

____

____

____

____

____

____

____

____

____

____

____

____

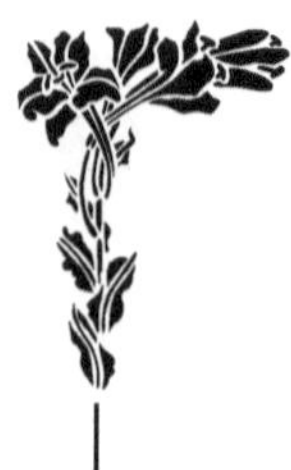

"Kind words can be short and easy to speak but their echoes are truly endless."

Mother Teresa

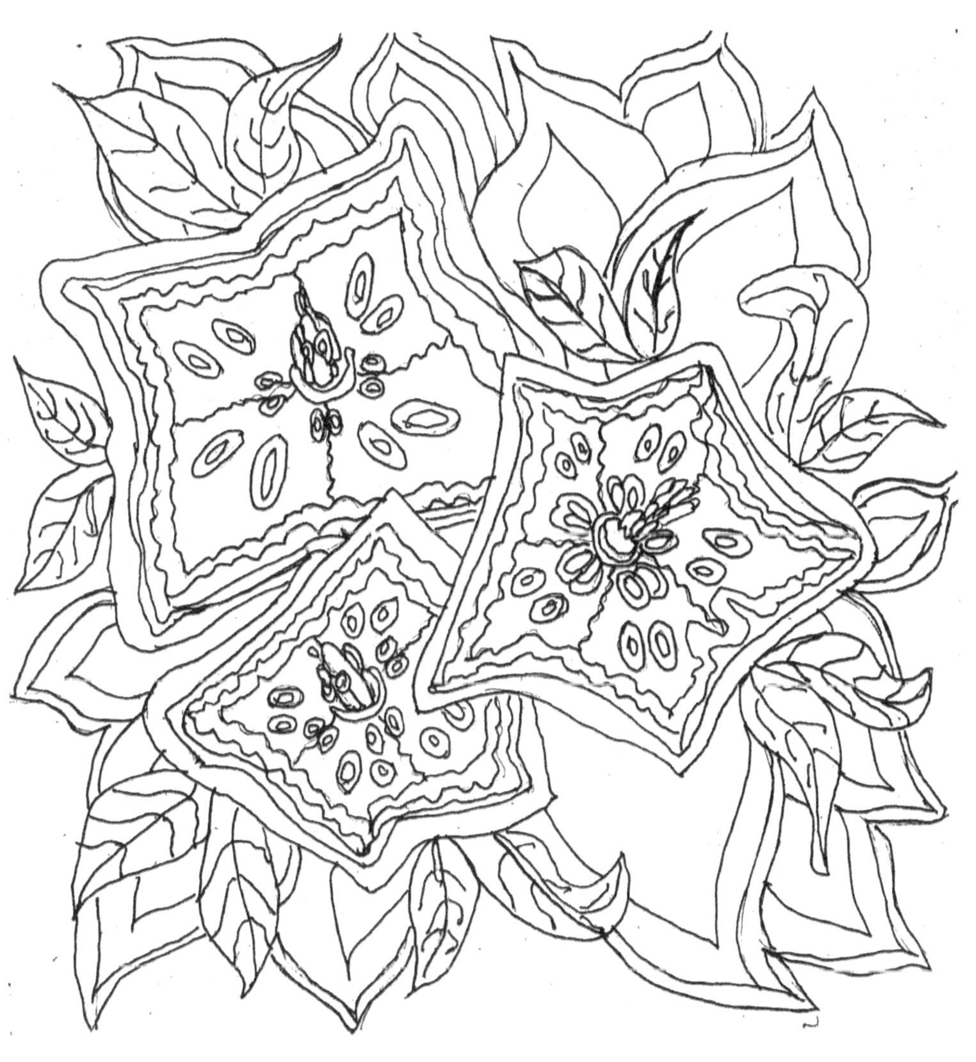

Question #20: What is the most creative thing you have done?

____

____

____

____

____

____

____

____

____

____

____

____

____

____

____

____

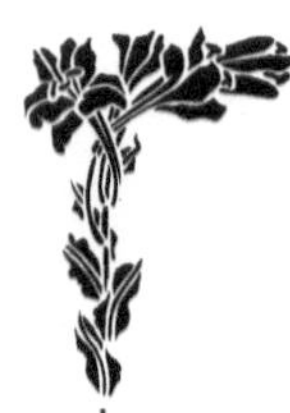

*"We must build dikes of courage
to hold back the flood of fear."*

Martin Luther King Jr.

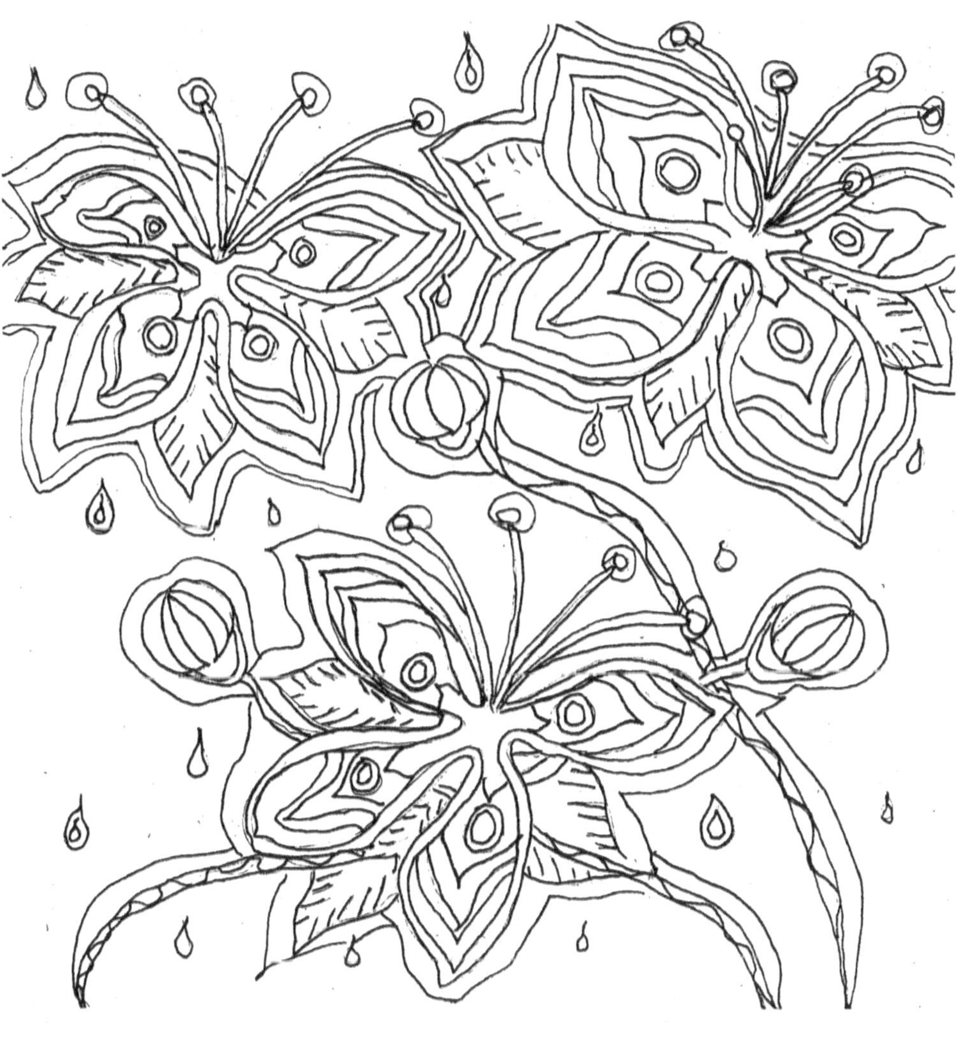

Question #21: What skill or skills do you want to learn/develop?

____

____

____

____

____

____

____

____

____

____

____

____

____

____

____

____

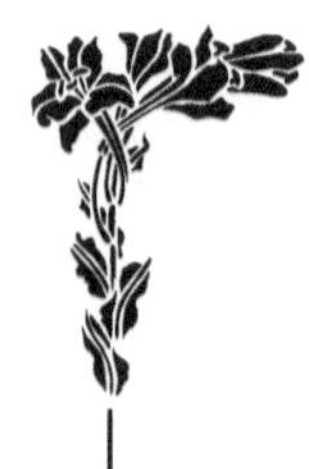

"Live as if you were
to die tomorrow. Learn as if
you were to live forever."

Mahatma Gandhi

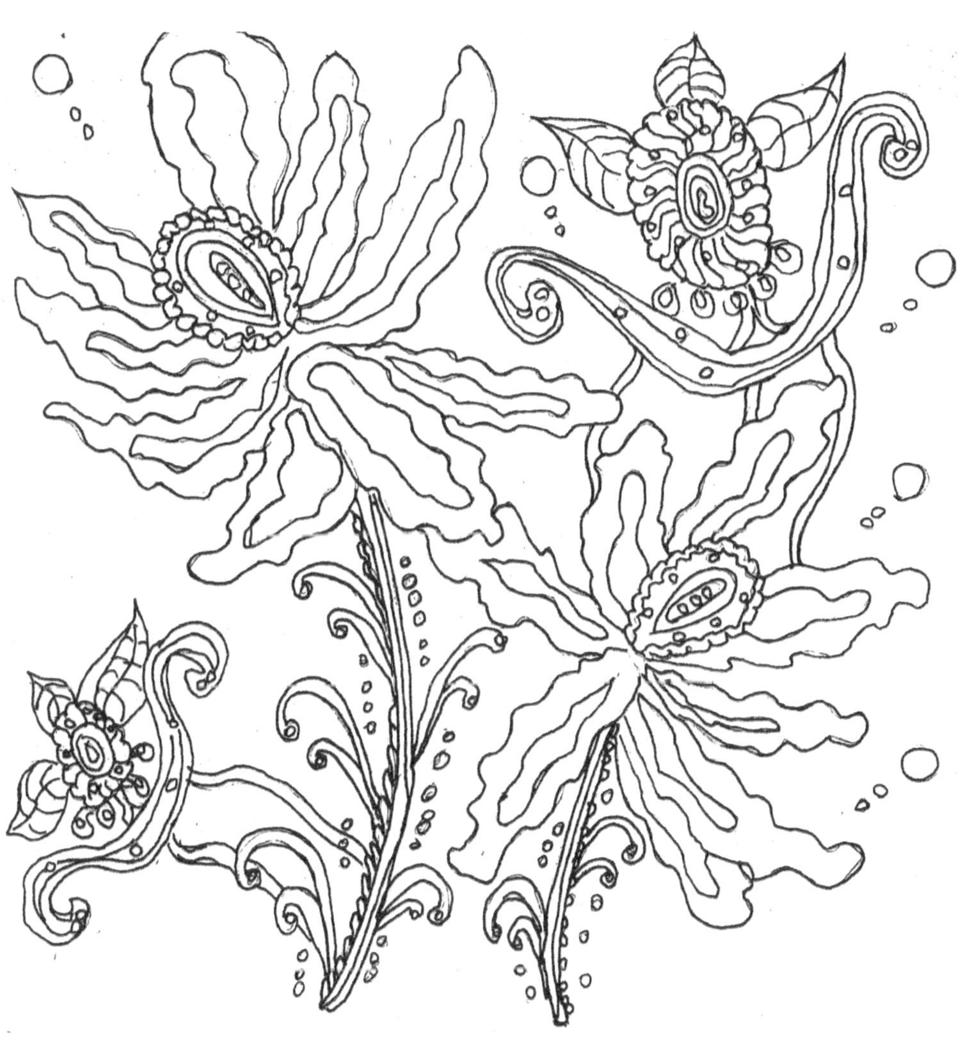

Question #22: What habit would you like to break, and replace?

____

____

____

____

____

____

____

____

____

____

____

____

____

____

____

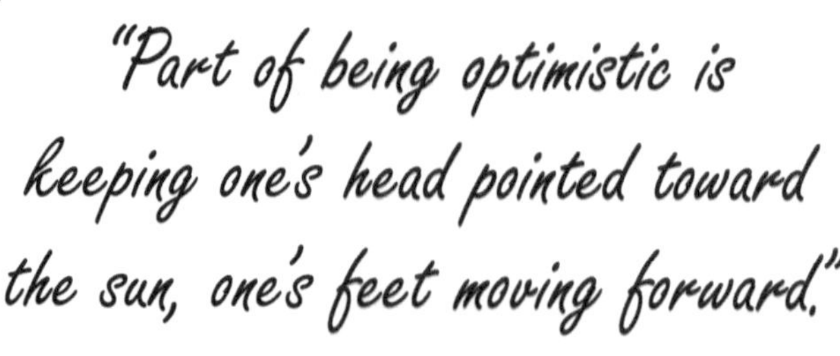

"Part of being optimistic is keeping one's head pointed toward the sun, one's feet moving forward."

Nelson Mandela

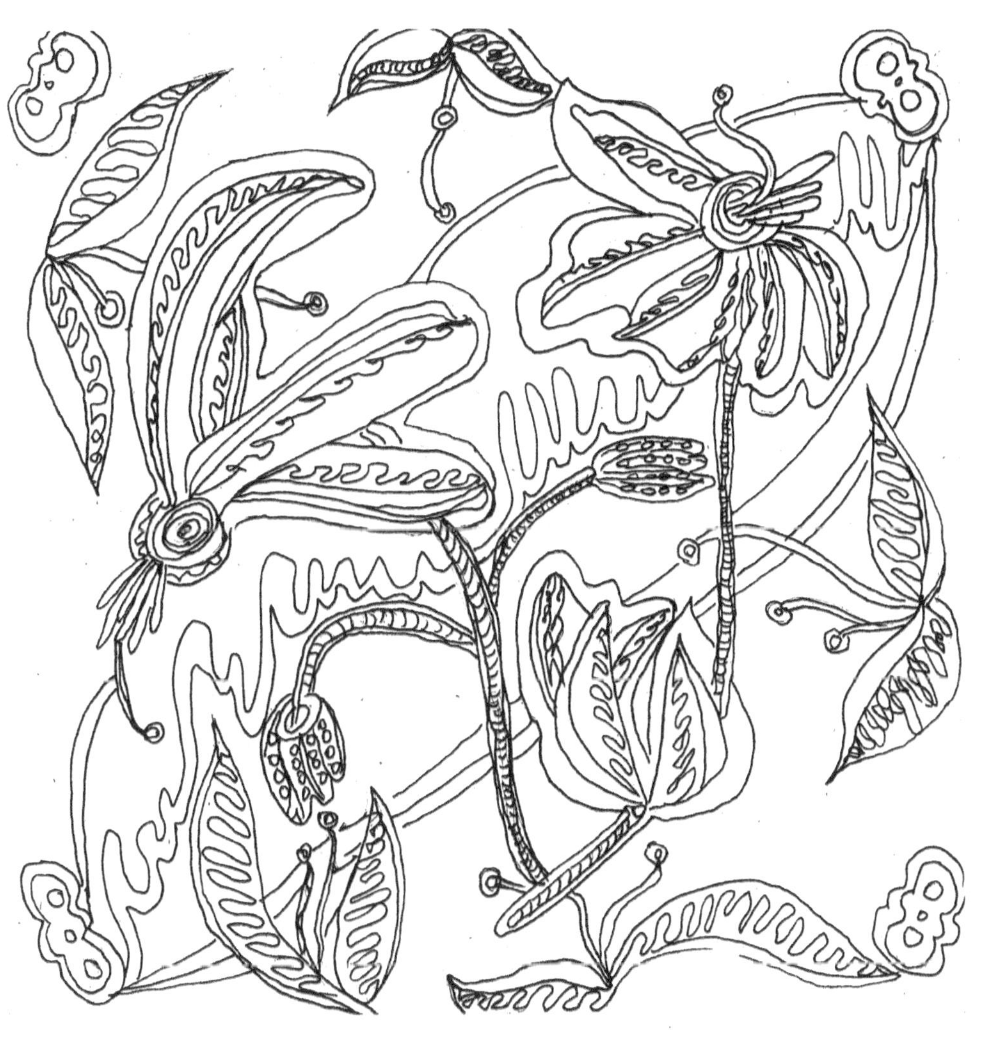

Question #23: What are some of your greatest strengths?

____

____

____

____

____

____

____

____

____

____

____

____

____

____

____

____

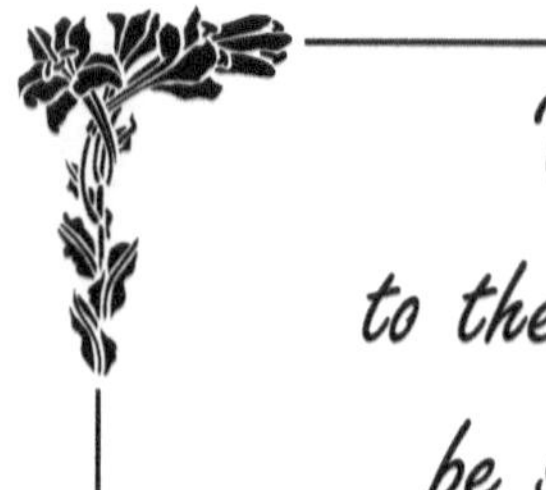

"Give careful thought to the paths for your feet and be steadfast in your ways."

Proverbs 4:26 NIV

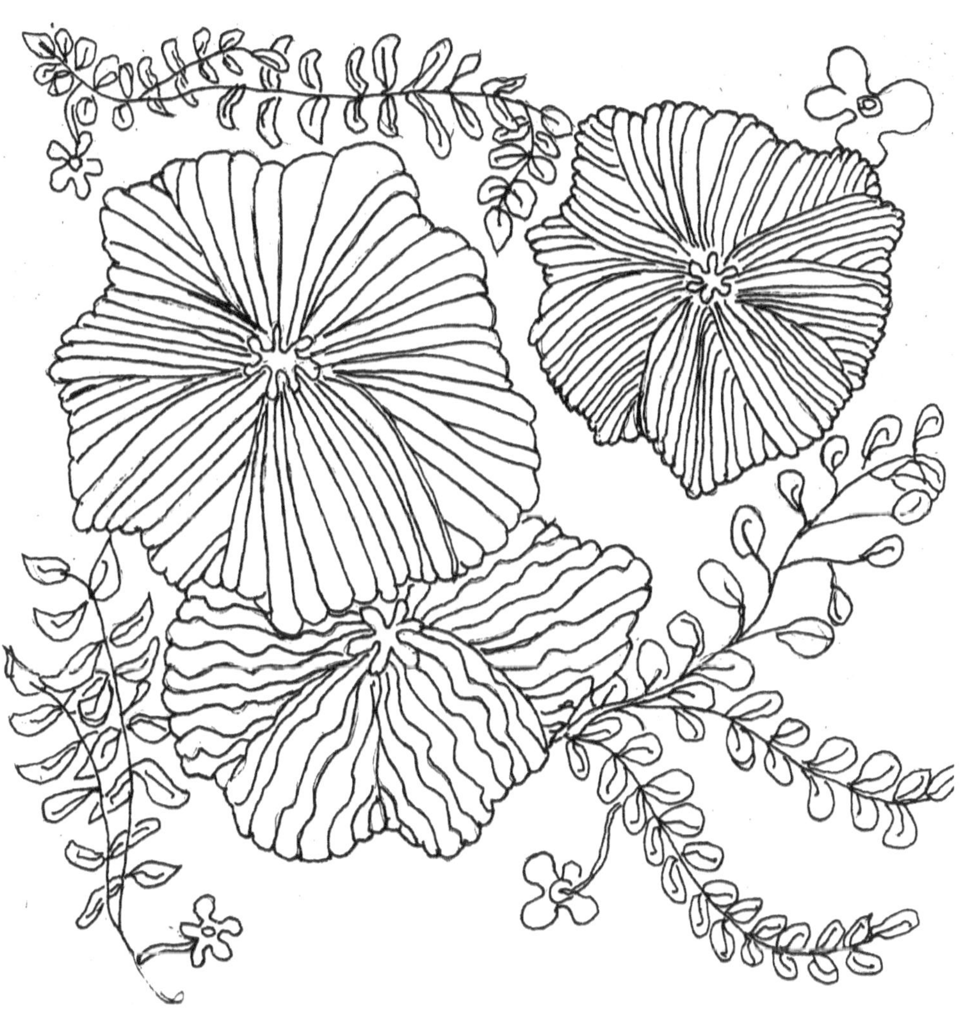

Question #24: Who could you call, write or send an encouraging word, letter or text to today?

____

____

____

____

____

____

____

____

____

____

____

____

____

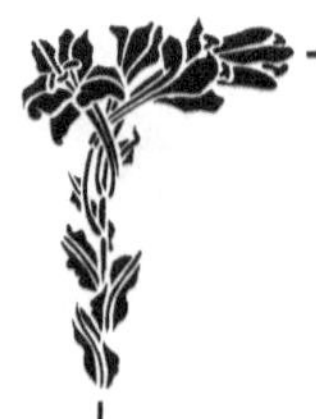

"Spread love everywhere you go.
Let no one ever come to you
without leaving happier."

Mother Teresa

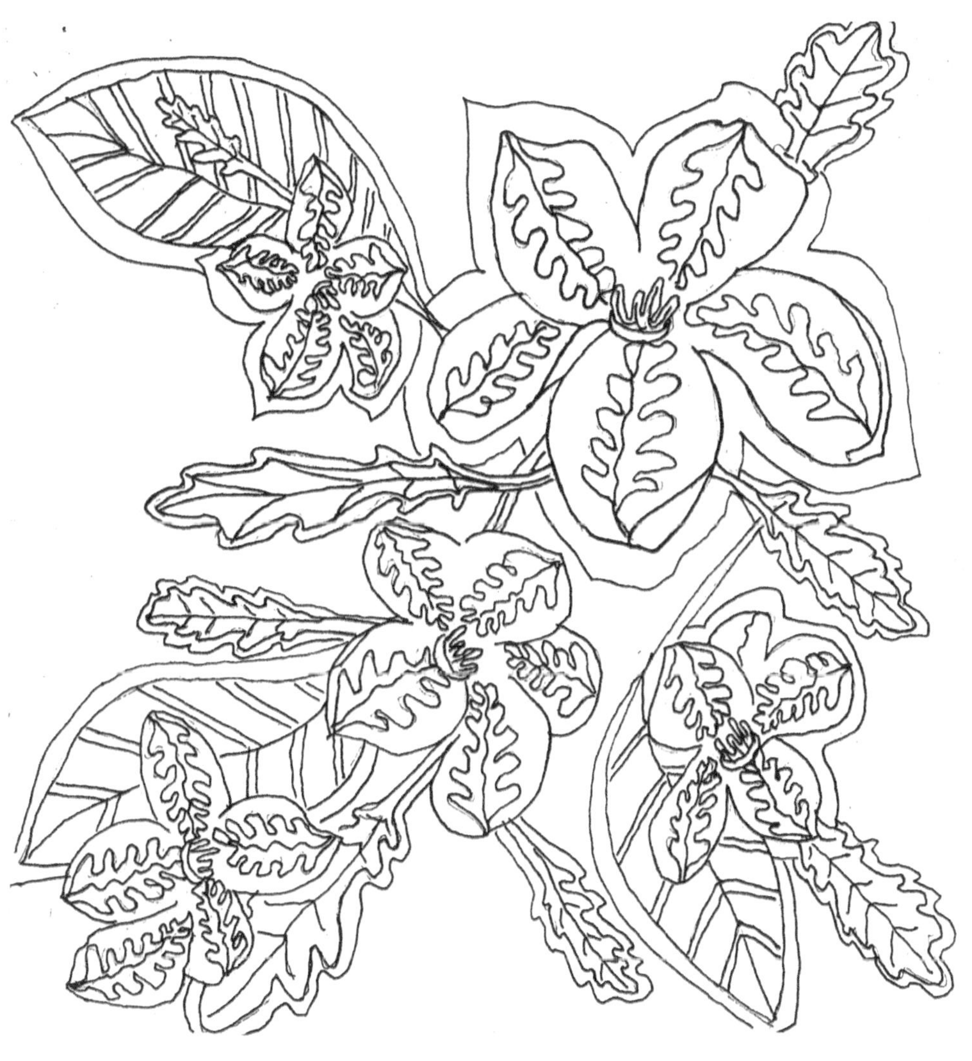

Question #25: What are your hopes for the next year?

____

____

____

____

____

____

____

____

____

____

____

____

____

____

____

____

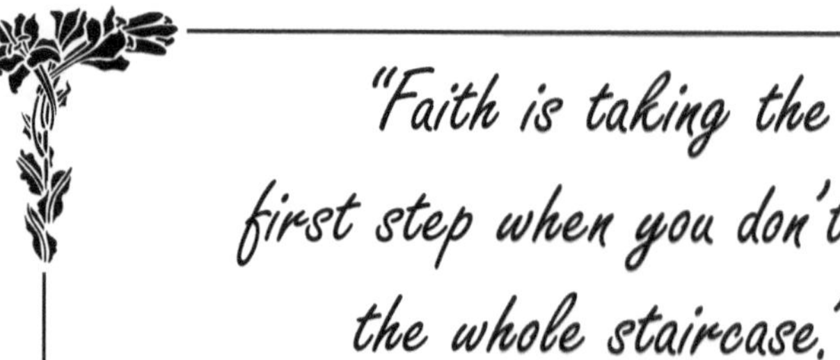

Martin Luther King Jr.

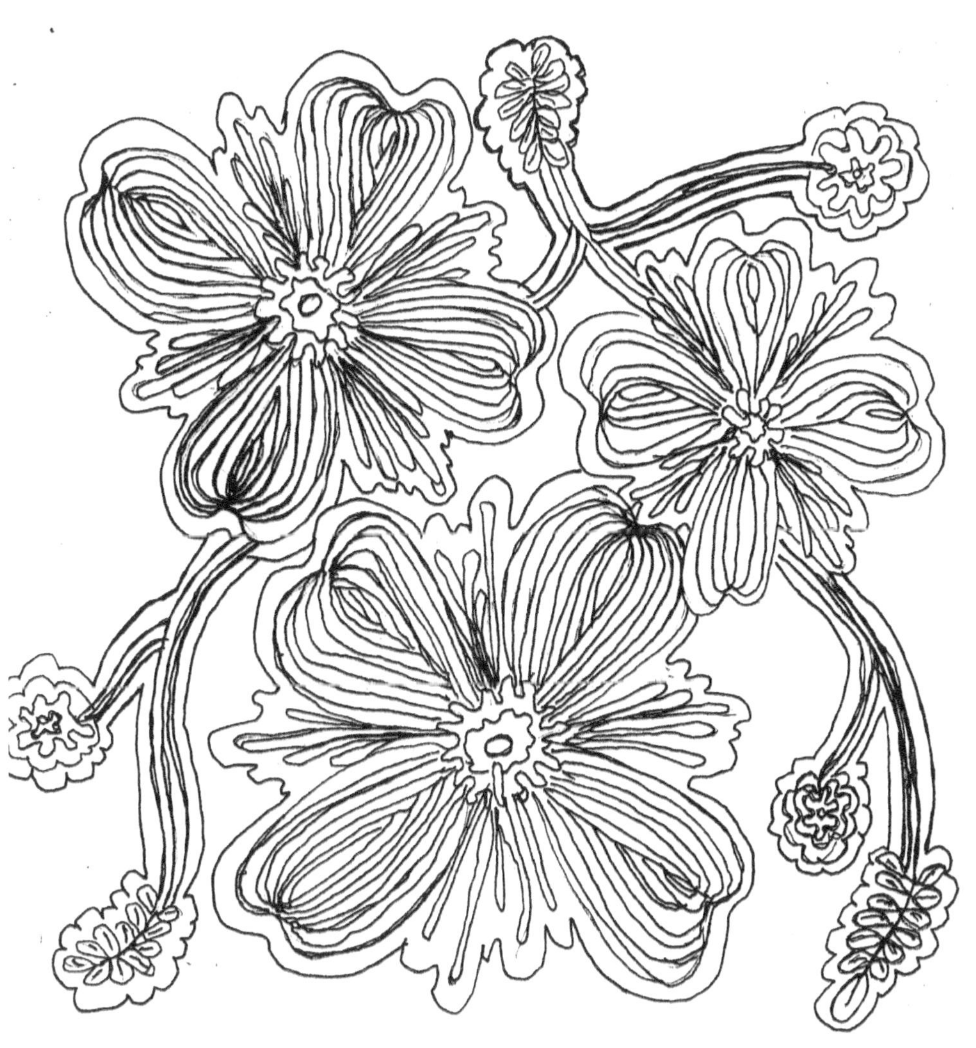

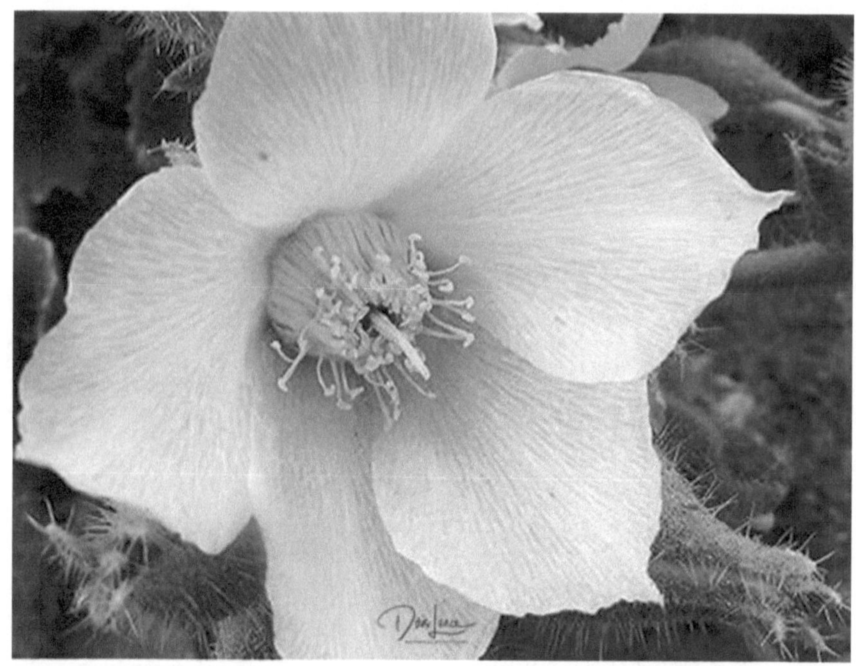

1

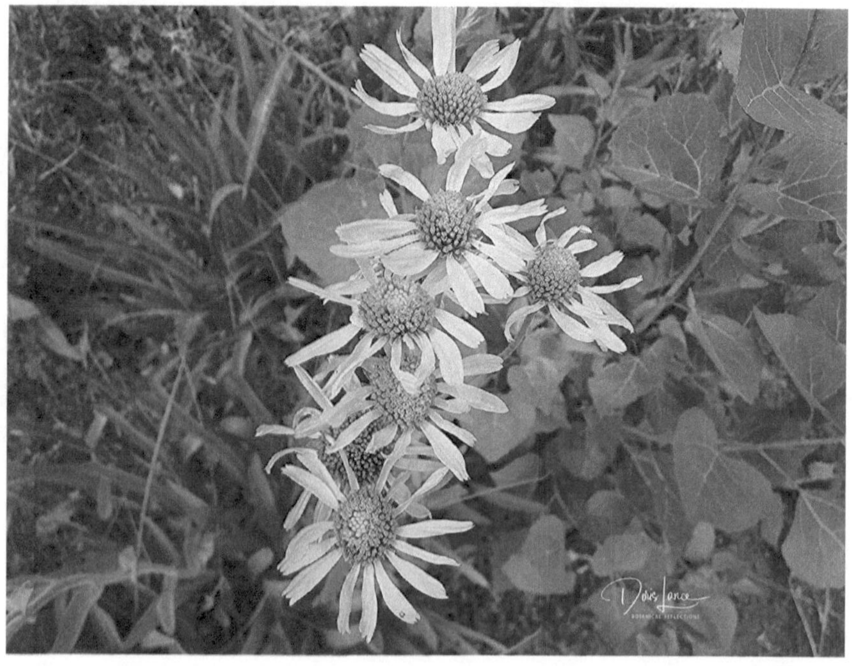

2

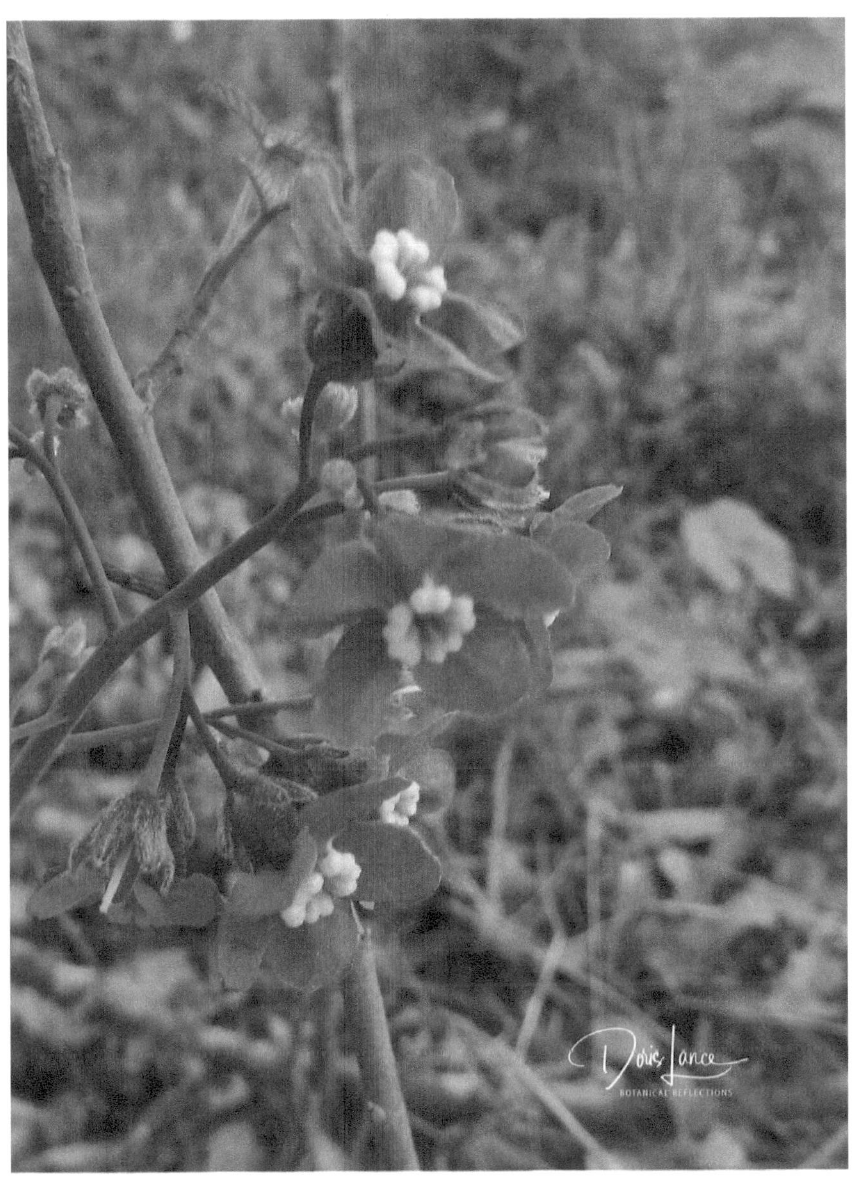

3

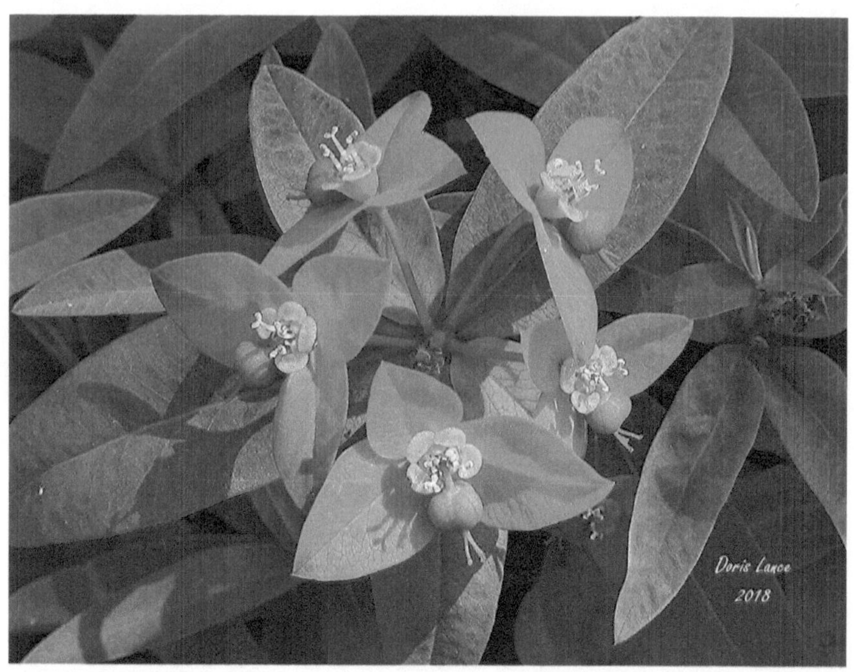

4

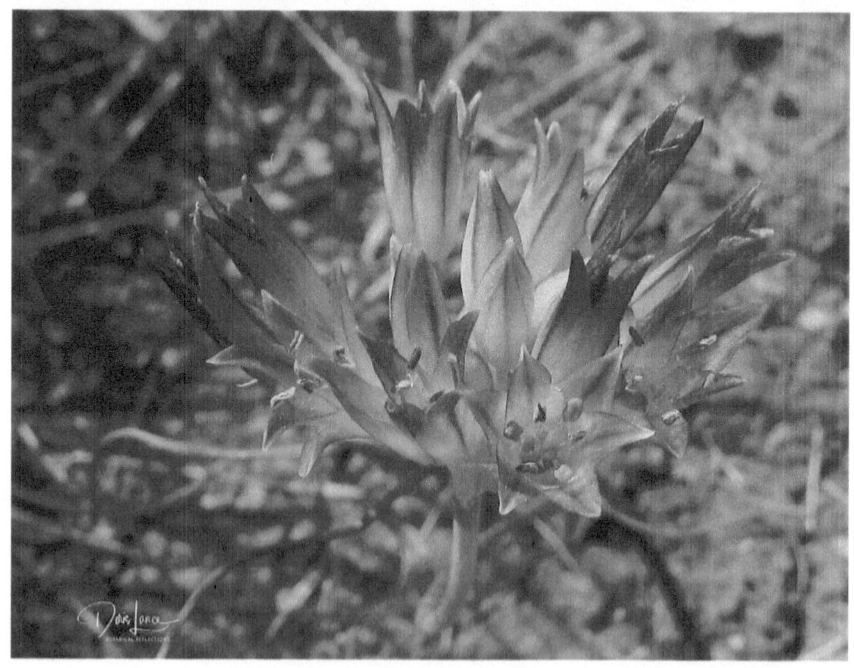

5

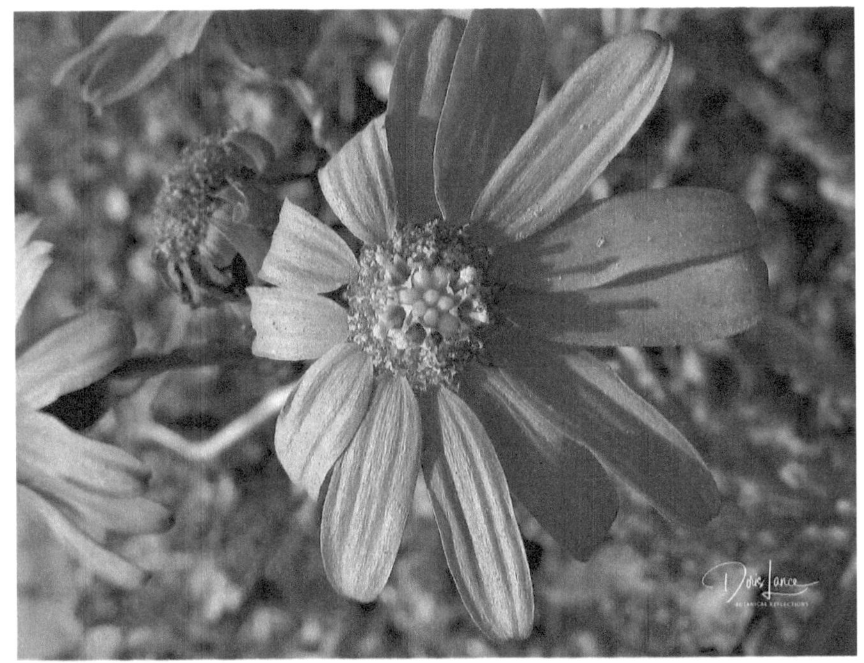

6

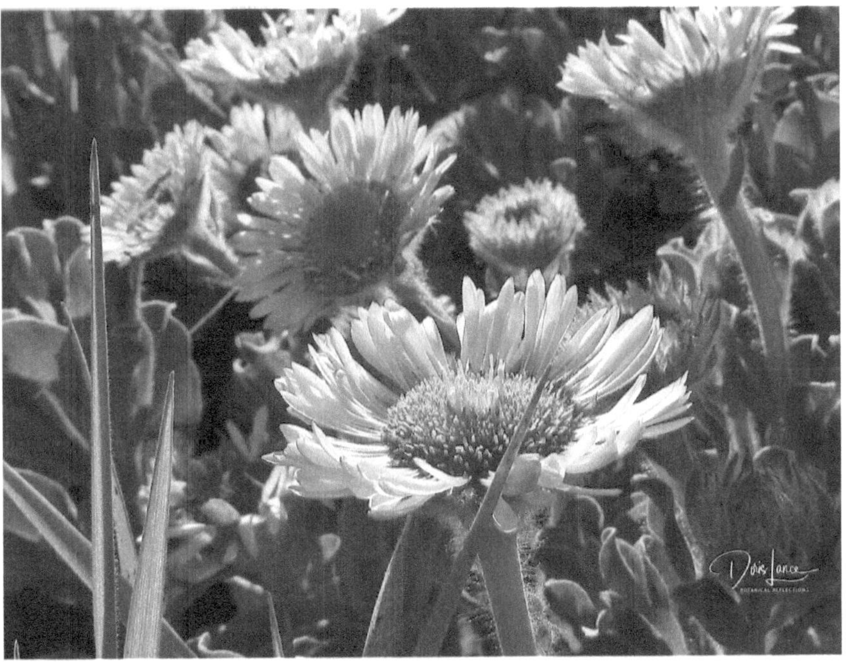

7

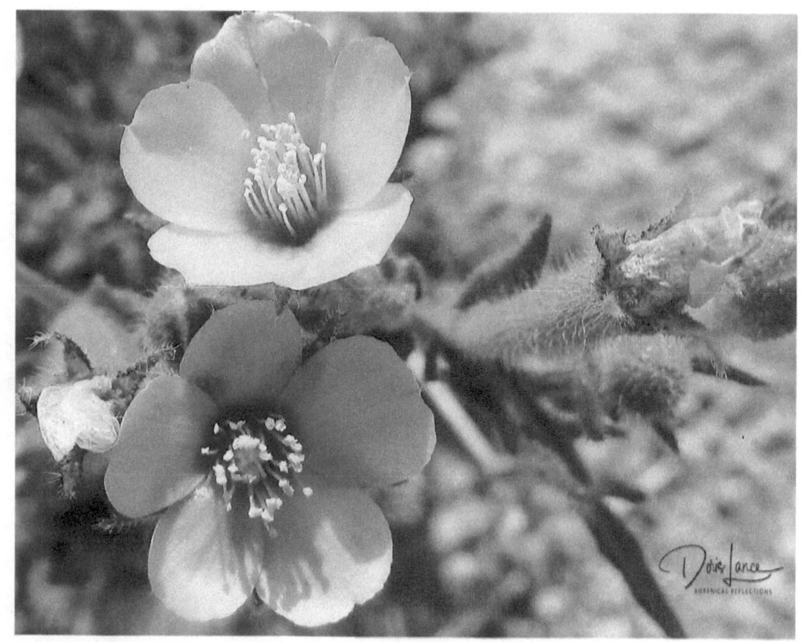

8

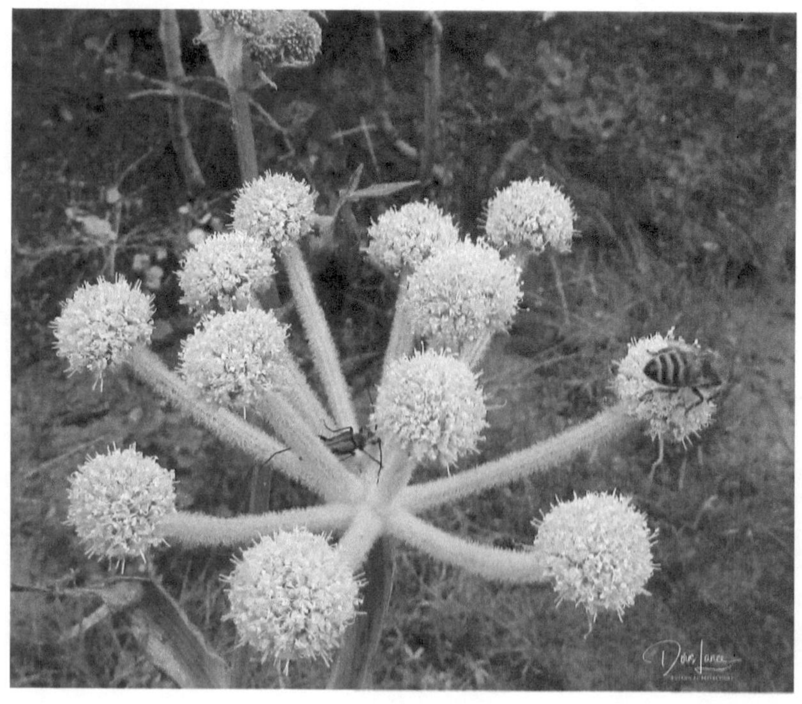

9

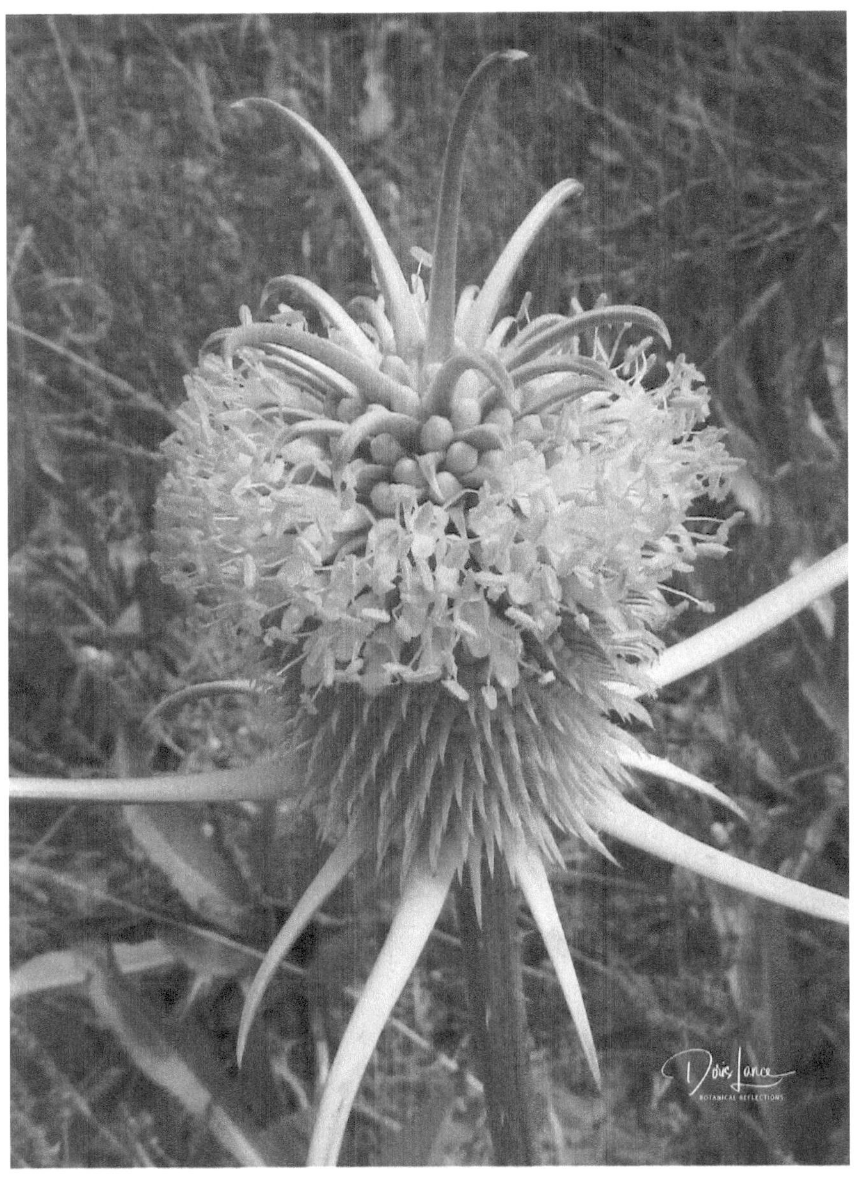

10

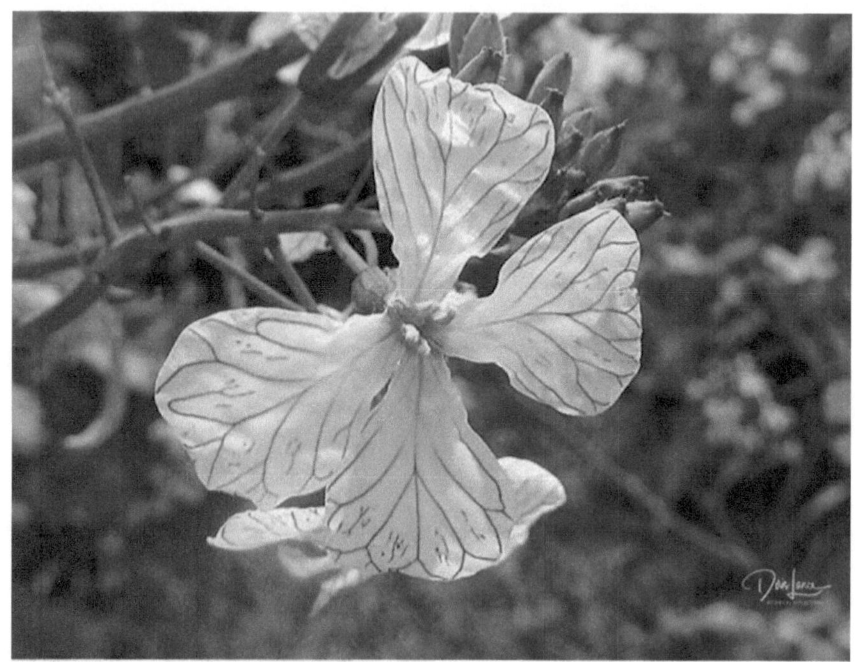

11

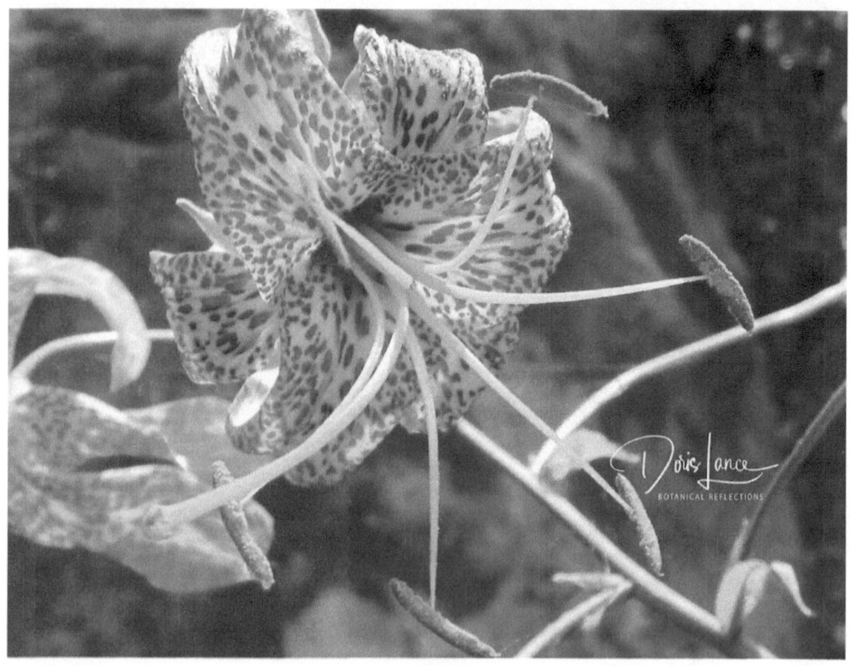

12

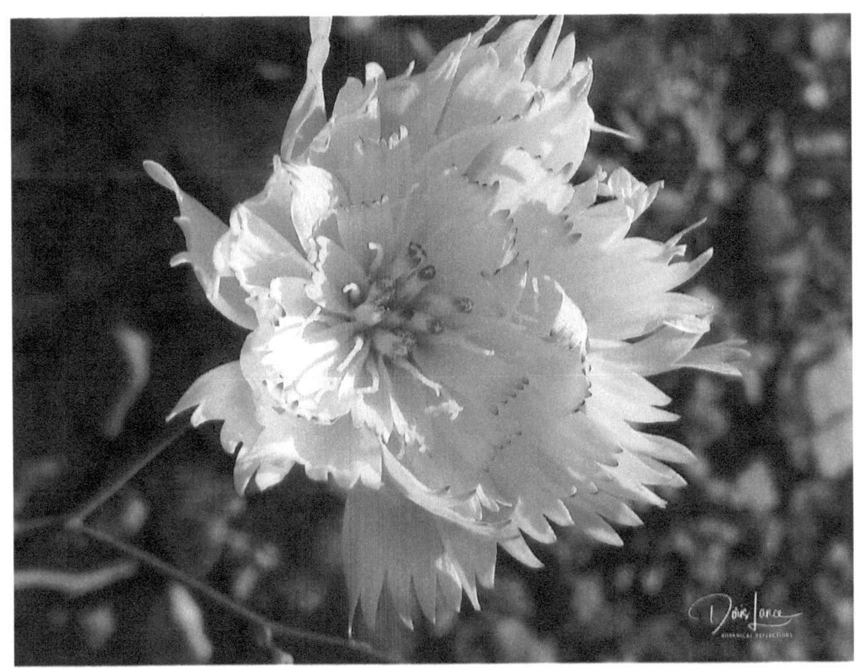

13

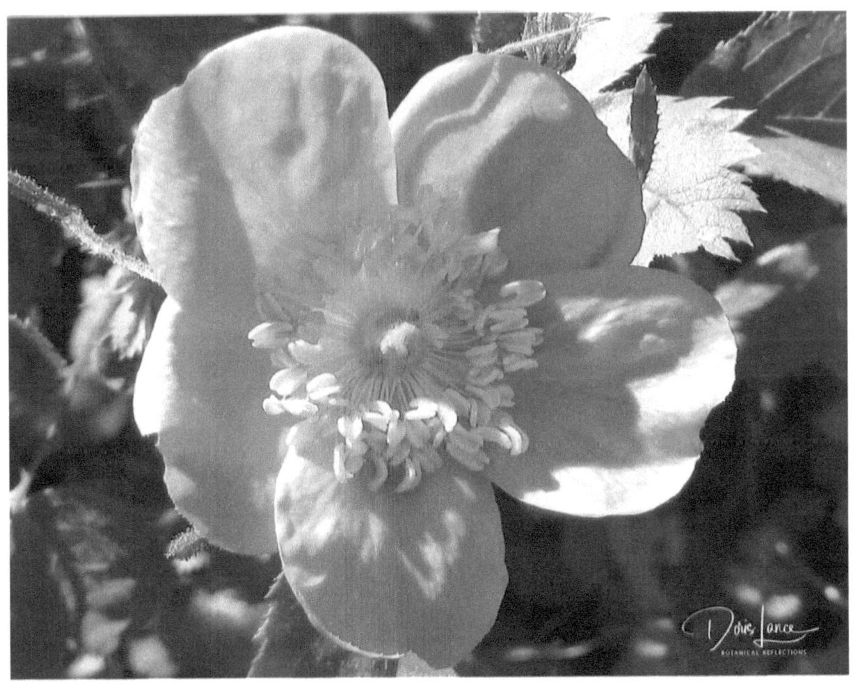

14

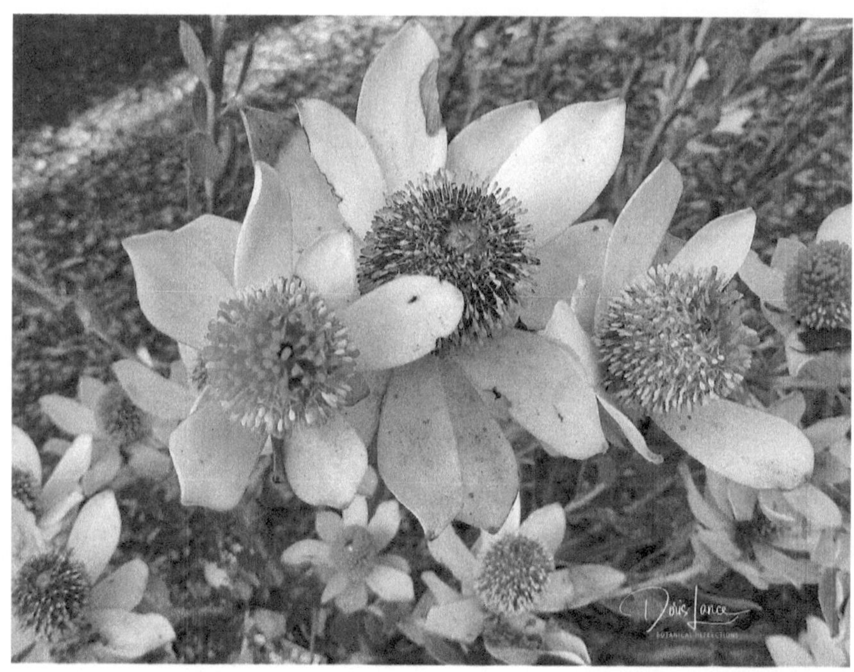

15

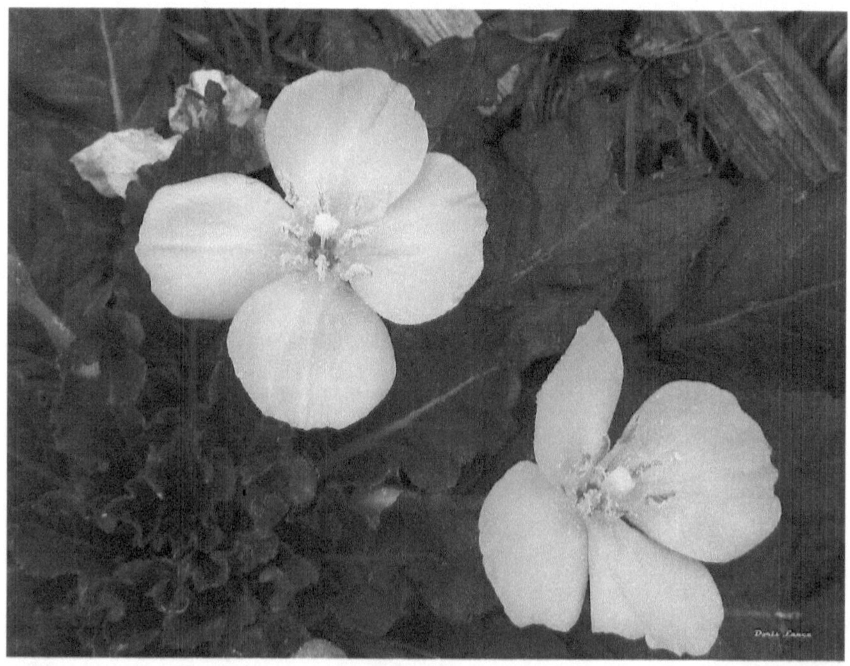

16

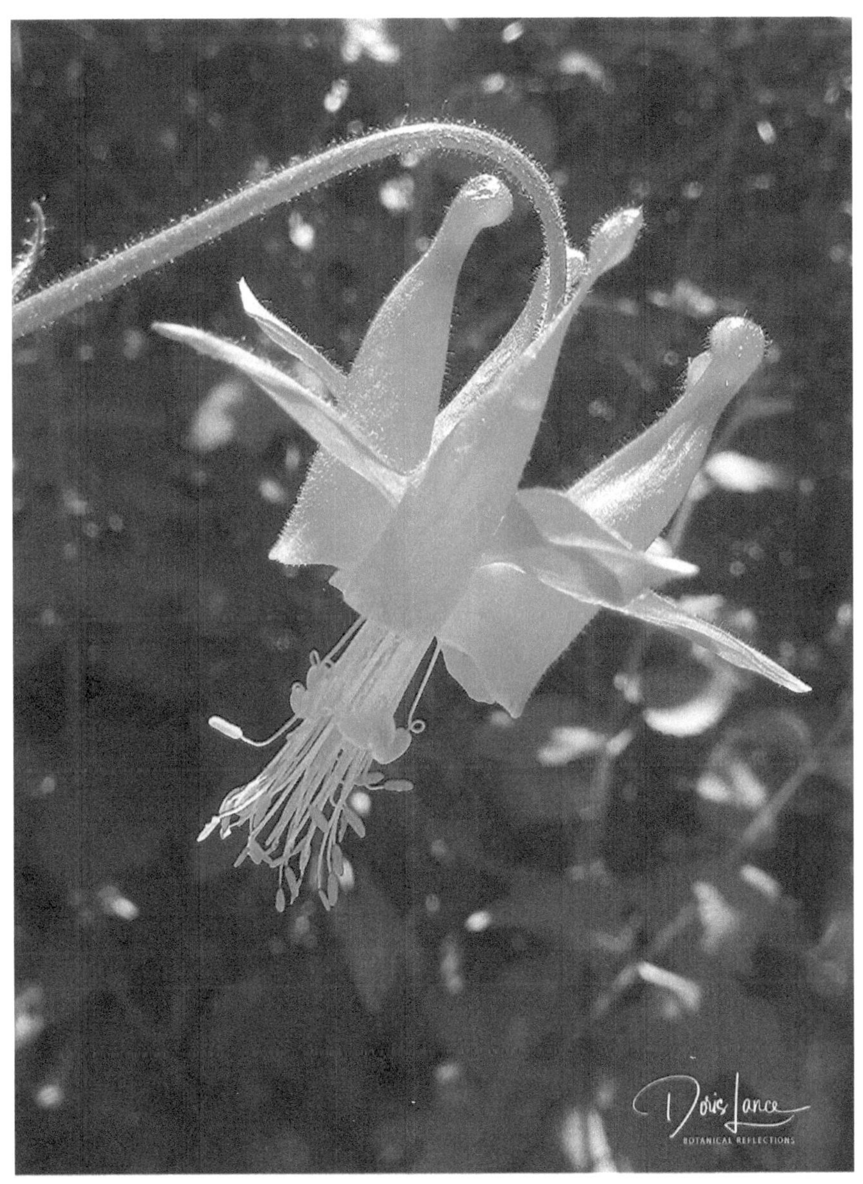

17

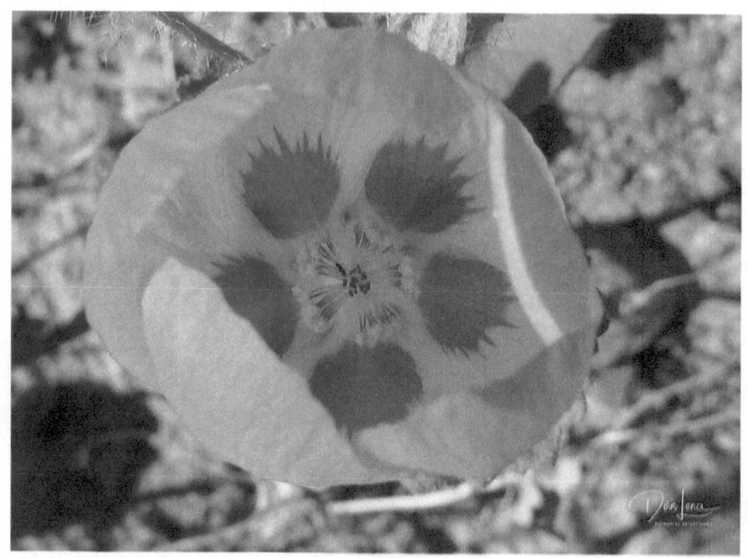

18

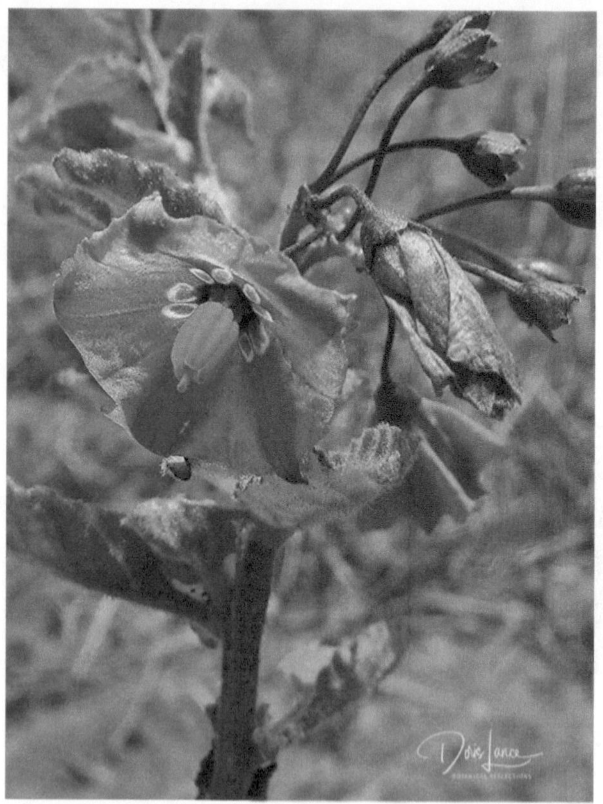

19

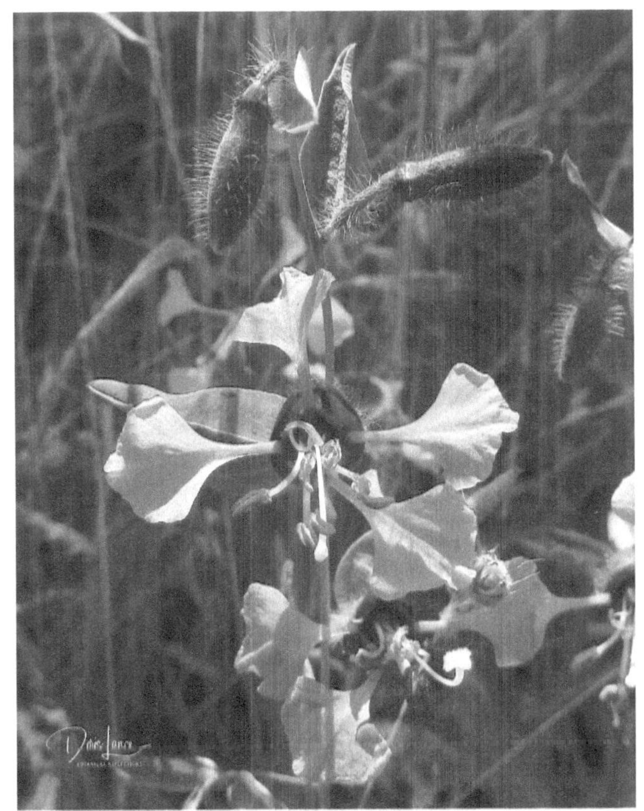

20

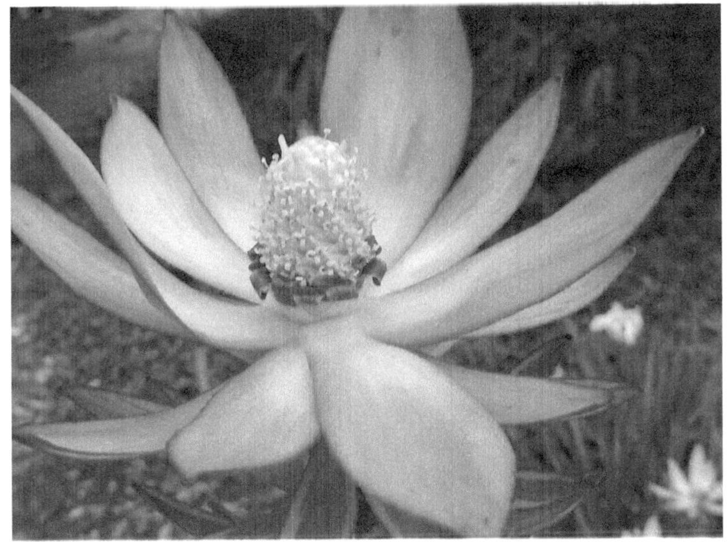

21

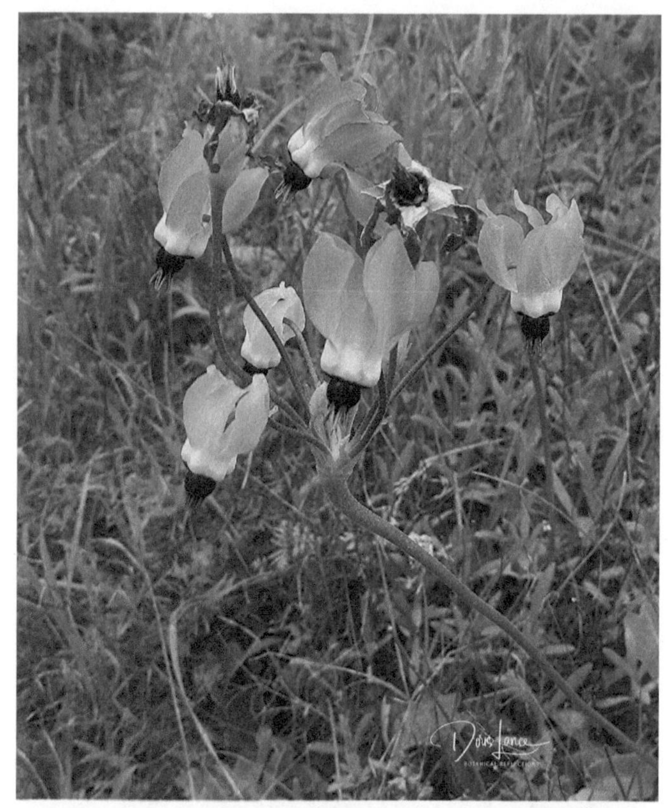

22

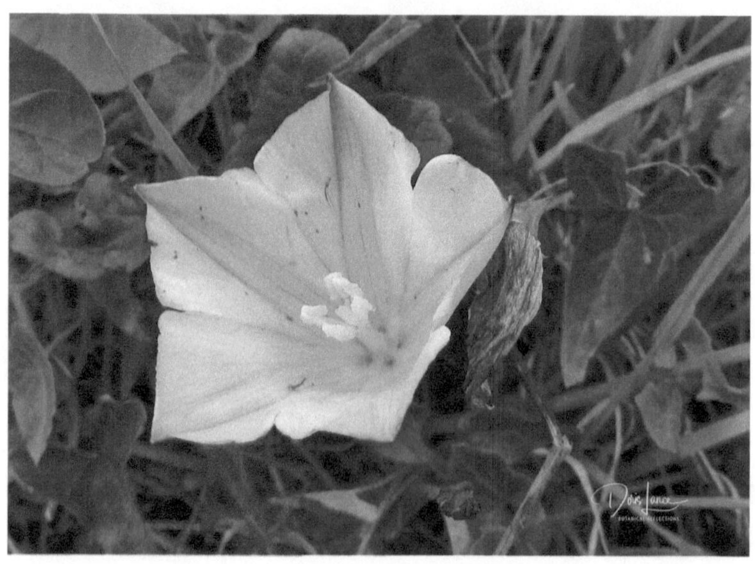

23

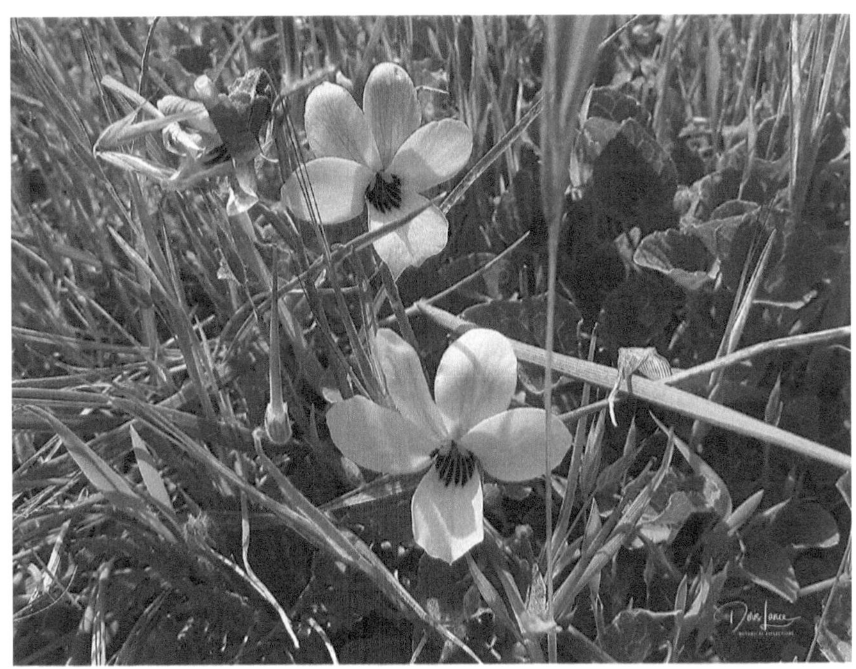

24

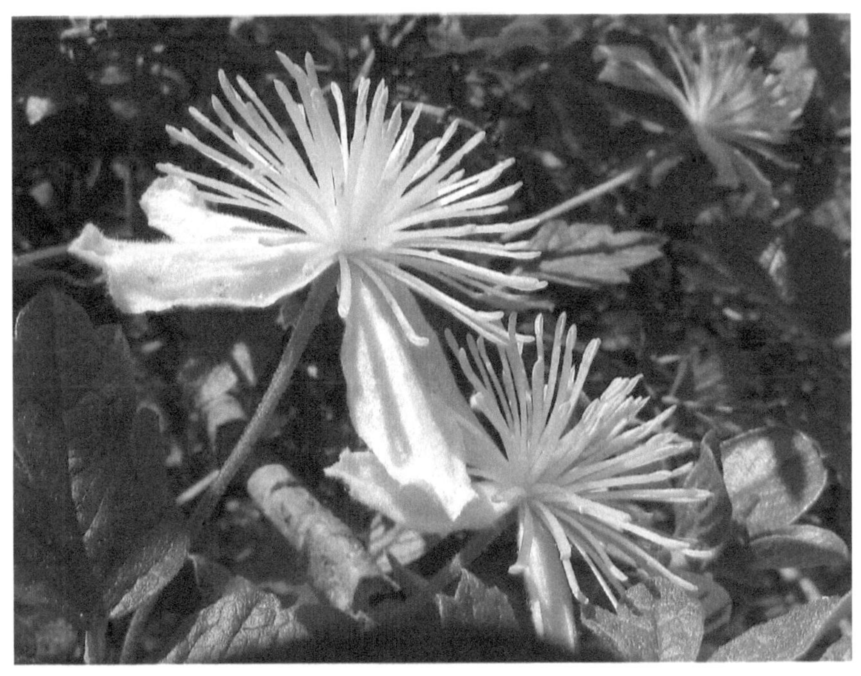

25

KEY IDENTIFICATION for WILDFLOWER SKETCHES BY AUTHOR DORIS LANCE

1. Rock Nettle-*Eucnide uerns*
2. Spearleaf arnica-*Arnica longifolia*
3. Grand Hounds tongue-*Cynoglossum grande*
4. Unknown from Edinburg Botanical Gardens, Scotland
5. One Leaf Onion-*Allium unifolium*
6. Common Sand Aster-*Corethrogyne filaginfolia*
7. Seaside Fleabane-*Erigeron glaucus*
8. Santa Lucia Stick leaf-*Mentzeliallll gracilente*
9. Rangers Buttons-*Sphenosciaduim capitellatum*
10. Fullers' Teasel-*Dispsacus fullonum*
11. Wild Radish-*Raphanus raphanistrum*
12. Leopard Lily-*Lilium pardalinum*
13. Desert Chicory-*Rafinesquia neomexicana*
14. California Wild Rose-*Rosa californica*
15. *Leucadendron gandogeri*
16. Beach Evening Primrose-*Camissoniopsis cheiranthifolia*
17. Crimson Columbine-*Aquilegia formosa*
18. Desert Five Spot-*Eremalche rotundifolia*
19. Blue Witch Nightshade-*Salanum umbelliferum*
20. Elegant Clarkia-*Clarkia unguiculata*
21. Pink Lotus-*Nelumbo nucifera*
22. Padre's Shooting Star-*Primula clevelandii*
23. Beach Morning Glory-*Calystegia soldanella*
24. Johnny Jump Up-*Viola pedunculata*
25. Chaparral Clematis-*Clematis lasiantha*

**All photographs are by the Author are copyrighted, and cannot be duplicated.